Martin Rosswog *Schultenhöfe*

Martin Rosswog

Schultenhöfe

Mit einem Text von Jan Carstensen

Schirmer/Mosel

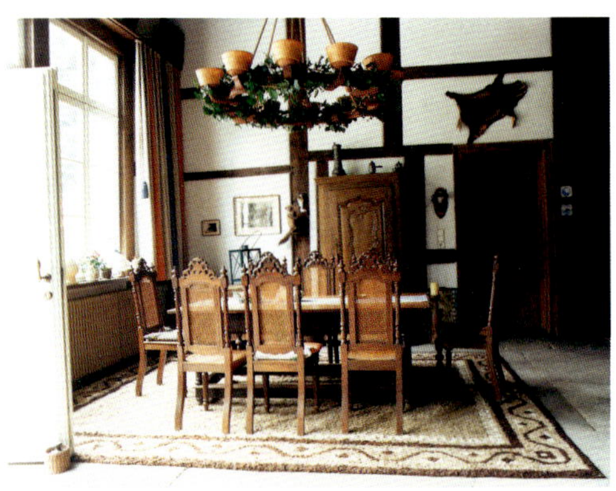
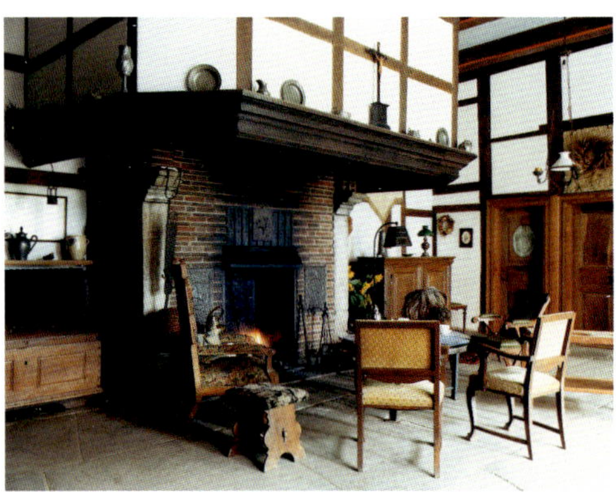
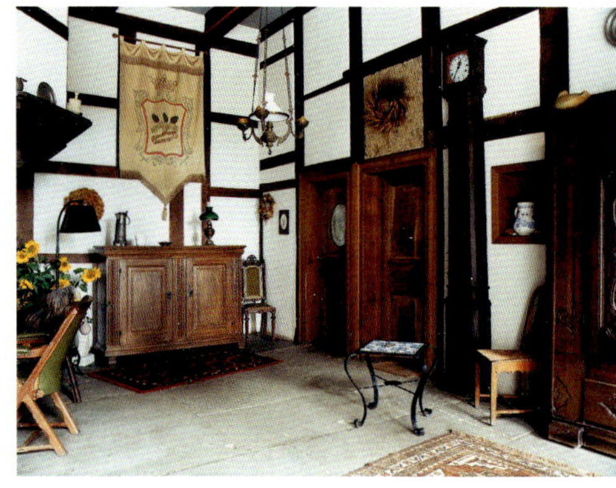
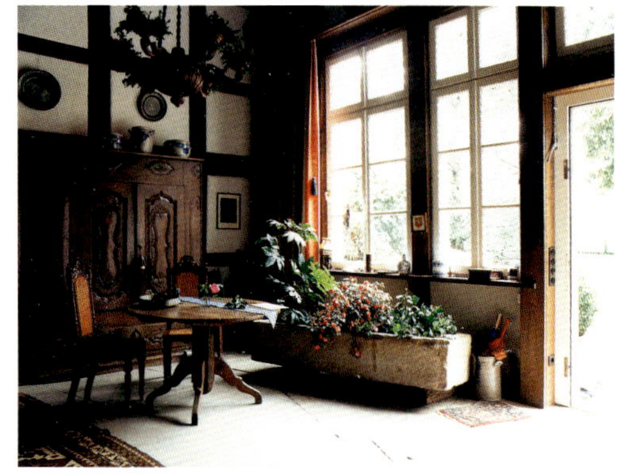

Martin Rosswog, Farbserie mit vier Innenaufnahmen, Hof C, 2000

Jan Carstensen

inside – mit Martin Rosswog unterwegs

Es war ein leicht bewölkter Maitag des Jahres 1999, die Landstraße von Münster zog sich gemächlich dahin. Ich suchte einen der großen Höfe dieses noch immer stillen Landstrichs mit seinen weitläufigen Feldern und seiner reizvollen, parkähnlichen Kulturlandschaft, die seit dem Mittelalter durch Landwirtschaft und einzeln gelegene Hofanlagen geprägt ist. Hinter einem kleinen Eichenwäldchen machte meine Straße eine scharfe Linkskurve, und plötzlich war ich da: direkt am Torhaus, das den Blick auf den Innenhof freigab, einsam, bis auf den mich freudig begrüßenden Hofhund und einen Citroën-Kombi mit rheinischem Kennzeichen. Martin Rosswog war – wie geplant – bereits vor Ort, und ich machte mich auf die Suche nach einem Klingelknopf, vergeblich, bis ich schließlich doch gesehen wurde und Einlass fand. So begann meine Entdeckungsreise zu den großen Bauernhöfen des Münsterlandes und ihren Bewohnern. Alles war so weit wie möglich vorbereitet. Wir hatten uns auf dem Hof brieflich und telefonisch für diesen Frühlingstag angemeldet. Die Gastfreundschaft der Bewohner tat ihr Übriges, um ein fotografisches Kunst- und Dokumentationsprojekt glücklich zu starten. Doch wie hatte alles begonnen?

Die erste Begegnung

Zurück in die 1980er Jahre zu meiner ersten Begegnung mit Martin Rosswog. Ich traf ihn in seinem Wohnort Lindlar im Oberbergischen Kreis. Vom ersten Moment an war ich von seinen Fotografien fasziniert, aber auch der Mensch Martin Rosswog beeindruckte mich sehr. Ich hatte zu dieser Zeit gerade meine Arbeit als Volkskundler am Bergischen Freilichtmuseum aufgenommen. Es war sicher die geradezu als volkskundlich zu bezeichnende Vorgehensweise Rosswogs, die mich anzog. Aber auch in seiner Beharrlichkeit, mit der er sein Ziel verfolgte, ohne auf den Kunstmarkt zu schielen, war er konsequent. In seiner näheren Umgebung hatte er zunächst Porträts fotografiert, die er kontinuierlich zu thematischen Serien ausbaute.[1] Später bereiste er ganz Europa auf der Suche nach traditionellen ländlichen Innenräumen, um sie nach festgelegten Aufnahmebedingungen und Prinzipien zu dokumentieren. Allein der deutschsprachige Raum blieb in dieser Hinsicht lange ausgeklammert. Im Bergischen Land konnten wir in den 1980er Jahren nur noch wenige Beispiele für »altertümliches« Wohnen gemeinsam entdecken.

Über zehn Jahre vergingen, ich war inzwischen ans Westfälische Freilichtmuseum nach Detmold gewechselt, Martin Rosswog hatte mit der gleichen Stetigkeit weitere Länder am Rande Europas bereist, als ich erneut Kontakt zu ihm aufnahm. Mittlerweile hatte ich das Thema Fotografie auch am Detmolder Museum zu einem Schwerpunkt ausgebaut. Ich hegte den großen Wunsch, in der Region Westfalen ein gemeinsames Projekt zu beginnen, und es gelang, Martin Rosswog dafür zu begeistern. Da uns ganz Westfalen mit seinen verschiedenen Teillandschaften für ein solches Vorhaben zu inhomogen erschien, konzentrierten wir uns auf das Münsterland und seine »Schultenhöfe«.

Schulten im Münsterland

Ein großer Bauer wird im Münsterland »Schulte« oder »Schulze« genannt – ein Begriff, den man im Lexikon vergeblich sucht. Schaut man hier allerdings ins Telefonbuch, findet sich »Schulte« als Name oder Namensteil sehr häufig. Nicht nur hier, im »Herzen Westfalens«, auch im nördlichen Ruhrgebiet und im Sauerland ist er verbreitet.[2] Die Bezeichnung »Schulte« (von altsächsisch »sculthetus«) tritt oft in zusammengesetzten Namen alter, großer Bauernhöfe auf, etwa Schulte-Bisping, Schulte des Bischofs. Ihr Ursprung ist im mittelalterlichen System der feudalen Grundherrschaft zu suchen, das erst im 19. Jahrhundert endgültig abgelöst wurde: Die Höfe waren kein freies Eigentum der Bauern, sondern gehörten adligen oder kirchlichen Grundherren, die sie durch vorwiegend leibeigene

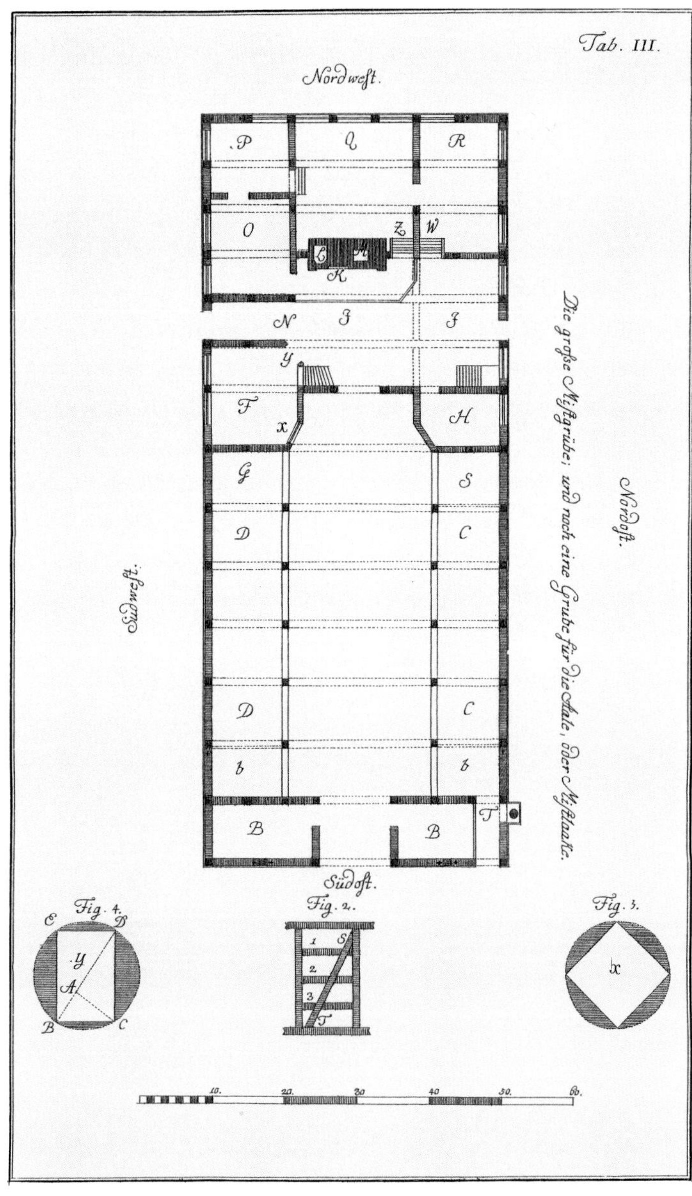

Idealentwurf eines stattlichen Bauernhauses des Münsterlandes, Kamin zwischen Kammern und Küche, hier schon vom großen Stallteil abgetrennt. Aus: Anton Bruchhausen: *Anweisung zur Verbesserung des Ackerbaues und der Landwirtschaft*… Münster 1790, Tafel III

Bauern bewirtschaften ließen. In Nordwestdeutschland war die Leibeigenschaft nicht so drückend wie in den Gebieten östlich der Elbe. Denn im Münsterland hatten die Bauern einen erblichen Anspruch auf den Hof, mussten aber Abgaben sowie Hand- und Spanndienste an ihren Grundherrn leisten. Als »Schulte« wurden im hohen Mittelalter die vom Grundherrn eingesetzten Besitzer großer Haupthöfe bezeichnet, deren Inhaber ursprünglich die Natural- und Geldabgaben der nachgeordneten kleineren Höfe einzuziehen hatten. Später wurde diese Funktion von der grundherrlichen Verwaltung übernommen, doch behielten die alten Schultenhöfe eine herausgehobene Stellung innerhalb der traditionellen ländlichen Gesellschaft. Das in Nordwestdeutschland verbreitete Anerbenrecht (die Höfe wurden ungeteilt an den ältesten, in manchen Regionen auch an den jüngsten Sohn weitervererbt, die anderen Geschwister mit Geld abgefunden), günstige Agrarkonjunkturen und vielfach moderate Abgabenlasten führten seit dem Beginn der frühen Neuzeit zur Entstehung einer reichen bäuerlichen Kultur in Westfalen.

Die stattlichen Hofanlagen und ihre oft reiche Ausstattung mit wertvollen Möbeln, Zinn und Textilien sind noch immer sichtbarer Ausdruck der früheren Bedeutung der zur ländlichen Oberschicht gehörenden Schulten. – Dieses Erbe wird bis heute in vielen Familien gepflegt und bewahrt.

Unser kleines Team[3] hatte sich zum Ziel gesetzt, zehn Familien aus der bäuerlichen Oberschicht zu finden, die noch heute in einem traditionellen westfälischen Bauernhaus, einem niederdeutschen Hallenhaus ähnlich dem Schultenhof im Westfälischen Freilichtmuseum wohnen. Aber schon bald stellten wir fest, dass die Bau- und Familiengeschichte der alten Höfe im Münsterland weitaus vielschichtiger, aber auch spannender ist, als wir erwartet hatten. In einem traditionellen Hallenhaus wohnen heute nur noch wenige Bauernfamilien.

Vom Bauernhaus zur Villa

Ausgangspunkt für die 1999 begonnene Arbeit waren die historischen Höfe des Freilichtmuseums. Die Herangehensweisen waren dabei unterschiedlich. Während es bei Martin Rosswog die scheinbar statischen Verhältnisse sind, die ihn immer wieder herausfordern, stellten sich für den Volkskundler im Museum zum Teil andere Fragen: Westfälische Bauern haben ein beachtliches Beharrungsvermögen, sagt man. Können wir aus den heute bestehenden Höfen Rückschlüsse auf ältere Zustände ziehen? Was ist das Besondere an der traditionellen Wohnkultur der Münsterländer Schulten? Ist die Präsentation des musealen Schultenhofes in allen Einzelheiten korrekt? Eine Dokumentation mit fotografischen Mitteln sollte der erste Schritt sein zu einem Forschungsprojekt zur Bau- und Wohnkultur der großbäuerlichen Höfe des Münsterlandes. Hier setzte auch das Interesse des Fotografen ein, sein künstlerisches Schaffen um die Gruppe dieser Schultenhöfe zu erweitern.

Ein anschauliches Beispiel ist der genannte Schultenhof im Freilichtmuseum[4]: Über eine Brücke und durch ein Torhaus aus Fachwerk betritt der Besucher den Hofplatz, der von dem großen, 1787 erbauten Haupthaus des Hofes Schulte-Bisping aus Alst bei Albersloh (südlich von Münster) beherrscht wird. Dieses mächtige, 42 m lange Gebäude ist ein niederdeutsches Hallenhaus, wie die in ganz Nordwestdeutschland verbreitete Form des Bauernhauses genannt wird: Es vereinigt Wohnung, Stallung und Erntebergung unter einem Dach. Durch ein giebelseitiges Tor gelangt man auf die große Dreschtenne, die in Westfalen »Deele« genannt wird. An beiden Seiten der Deele liegen die Ställe für Kühe und Pferde; auf dem riesigen Dachboden darüber wird die Getreideernte gelagert. Am Ende der Deele schließt sich der Wohnteil des Hauses mit einer großen Küche an, die ursprünglich nicht durch Wände vom Stallteil getrennt war. Im Zentrum liegt die offene Herdstelle, die im Münsterland nach adligem Vorbild zu einem prächtigen Wandkamin mit großem Rauchfang ausgestaltet wurde. In vielen Bauernhäusern des Münsterlandes blieb dieses »Herdfeuer« (das schon lange nicht mehr zum Kochen genutzt wird) als traditioneller Mittelpunkt des Hauses bis heute erhalten. Da die Zugluft des Schornsteins den beliebten Platz am Herdfeuer ungemütlich machte, begann man vielfach schon im 18. Jahrhundert, die Kaminküche durch eine große Flügeltür oder eine Trennwand, Windfang genannt, von der Deele abzutrennen. So entstanden die typischen geräumigen Kaminküchen der westfälischen Bauernhäuser mit dem traditionellen Essplatz neben der Feuerstelle, der durch große Fenster viel Licht erhielt. Hinter der Herdstelle lagen weitere Stuben und Kammern am Ende des Hauses; Seitentüren führten von der Küche in den Garten und zum Brunnen. Hier befanden sich auch weitere Nebengebäude des Hofes wie Backhaus, Holzschuppen und Kornspeicher.

Die meisten Schulten errichteten im 19. Jahrhundert ein moderneres Wohnhaus, das entweder an das Hallenhaus angebaut wurde oder dieses gänzlich ersetzte. Grundlegend für diese Entwicklung war das wachsende Bedürfnis nach einer Trennung von Wohnen und Wirtschaften. Hatte man sich im ausgehenden 18. Jahrhundert noch mit einer Trennwand begnügt, begannen später die größeren Bauern, Flügelbauten aus Fachwerk oder zweigeschossige Backsteinwohnhäuser an ihre alten Hallenhäuser anzubauen. Um die Wende zum 20. Jahrhundert entstanden schließlich großzügige Villen im Historismus und Jugendstil, die dem gewachsenen Prestigebedürfnis der wohlhabenden großbäuerlichen Schicht entsprachen. Auch im 20. Jahrhundert wurden stattliche, »standesgemäße« Neubauten errichtet, die manchmal an städtische Unternehmervillen oder ländliche Herrenhäuser erinnern.

Als sich unser Projekt dem Ende näherte, hatten wir die wesentlichen Entwicklungsschritte vom Hallenhaus zur ländlichen Villa im Münsterland erfasst. Wir entschlossen uns, als zehntes und letztes Beispiel ein Gebäude aus der Gegenwart zu wählen, um nicht an einem beliebigen Punkt der historischen Entwicklung stehen zu bleiben. So wurde auch ein Haus aus dem Jahr 1995 dokumentiert. Damit wurde die Entwicklung auch baulich bis in die Gegenwart verfolgt. Zudem waren durch das ererbte Mobiliar in dem modernen Haus sogar noch ältere Wohnformen ablesbar.

Gegenwart im Museum

Parallel zum Schultenhof-Projekt hatte das Freilichtmuseum mit der Erforschung der Wohnkultur der Gegenwart begonnen: Unter dem Titel »ZimmerWelten – wie junge Menschen heute wohnen« dokumentierten wir das aktuelle Wohnen der jungen Generation anhand ihrer dinglichen Umwelt an der Wende zum 21. Jahrhundert; das Ergebnis war eine bundesweit beachtete Ausstellung im Jahr 2000.[5] Interessanterweise traten beim Vergleich der Kinder- und Jugendzimmer aus beiden Projekten viele Ähnlichkeiten zutage.

Im Unterschied zu dem Projekt »ZimmerWelten«, in das viele junge Menschen einbezogen waren, stehen mit den Schultenfamilien systematische Interviews noch aus. Dennoch gibt es eine Gemeinsamkeit: Es geht um das Wohnen in der Gegenwart und darum, wie dieses für die Nachwelt aussagekräftig dokumentiert werden kann. Im Vordergrund steht dabei weniger das statistische Grundlagenmaterial als vielmehr das Bemühen, aus der Vielfalt eine Wahl zu treffen, die möglichst die ganze Breite der Erscheinungsformen umfasst. Dass dabei eine gewisse Willkür nicht auszuschließen ist und nicht zuletzt auch die Bereitschaft der beteiligten Familien eine wichtige Rolle spielt, soll hier nicht verschwiegen werden. Die Auswahl fand im Gespräch zwischen Künstler und Wissenschaftler statt. Kriterien waren die Hausformen, in denen die Schultenfamilien leben, und nicht zuletzt der Wunsch des Museums, einen möglichst tiefen Einblick in das derzeitige Wohnen einer traditionellen ländlichen Sozialschicht zu gewinnen.

Mit seiner künstlerischen Akribie und Hartnäckigkeit hat Rosswog ein visuelles Gedächtnis der europäischen Wohnkultur geschaffen, das einzigartig dasteht. So zeigen seine Serien ein beispielhaftes Repertoire an jeweils neuen Möbeln und Wohnausstattungen zwischen 1930 und der Gegenwart, in die ältere »Erbstücke« eingebunden sind. Bisher wurden solche Milieus der zweiten Hälfte des 20. Jahrhunderts kaum im Lebenszusammenhang dokumentiert oder gar systematisch für die Nachwelt in Originalzeugnissen gesammelt – eine wichtige Aufgabe für die kulturhistorischen Museen. Aber nicht nur das volkskundlich-museale Interesse am Werk Martin Rosswogs ist beachtlich, auch nach seinem Vorgehen und seinen Methoden ist zu fragen.

Die fotografischen Serien

»Der Fotograf Martin Rosswog ist ein künstlerischer Dokumentarist.« So beginnt Andreas Graf seine Einleitung zu dem bislang umfassendsten Buch über Rosswogs Fotografien ländlicher Innenräume in Europa.[6] Sehr genau beschreibt Graf die Arbeitsweise und das Vorgehen des Fotografen: Eine erste Reise führte Rosswog 1989 nach Irland, wohin er in den folgenden Jahren noch einige Male zurückkehrte. Es folgten 1992 Spanien und 1995 Finnland, auch hier nutzte er weitere Besuche, um seine Serien zu ergänzen. Zutreffend wird das Interesse Rosswogs an »kulturellen Inseln« beschrieben.[7] Auch die Schultenhöfe lassen sich im Hinblick auf ihre Einzellage in der weiten, sie umgebenden Landschaft und ihre soziale Stellung inselartig auffassen.

Solche »kulturellen Inseln« haben auch Bernd und Hilla Becher, deren Meisterschüler Rosswog war, stets interessiert. Das Verhältnis zu ihrem Werk macht deutlich, wo Gemeinsamkeiten liegen, aber auch, wo Rosswog einen anderen Weg beschreitet. Die bekannten Becherschen Tableaus mit Fotografien von Fachwerkhäusern sind sehr genau erkundet.[8] Ein wesentlicher Teil des künstlerischen Schaffens ist die Anordnung der Fotografien, in der die Bedeutung des einzelnen Bildes zurücktritt.[9] Ähnliches ist auch bei den Schultenhöfe-Arbeiten Rosswogs zu beobachten. Während jede einzelne Innenaufnahme von volkskundlicher Seite zunächst als Bereicherung der Forschungsgrundlage gewertet wird, belässt er es nicht dabei, sondern fügt Bild und Bild aneinander und legt genau fest, welche zwei, drei, vier oder fünf Aufnahmen zusammengehören und welche mit gebührendem Abstand, aber dennoch zugehörig, gehängt werden sollen. Während die Tableaus der Bechers beispielsweise neun Aufnahmen mit je drei Bildern neben- und drei untereinander umfassen können, sind es bei Rosswog Serien aus zwei bis sechs Aufnahmen, auch 2 + 3 oder 5 + 1 Fotografien hat er zusammengestellt. Einzelbilder sind oft sehr stark zentrierte Aufnahmen oder Details, die sich der Serie entziehen. Die Serien sind nicht beliebig, sondern beinhalten optische Überschneidungen, so dass man beim genauen Hinsehen, die »Anschlusspunkte« entdecken kann. Die Verbindungen untereinander werden durch Möbel oder Türen und Fenster hergestellt, indem diese aus verschiedenen Perspektiven und angeschnitten in den Fotografien erscheinen. So ist es aber dennoch möglich und von Rosswog auch so gedacht, dass etwa aus einer Serie mit fünf auch eine kleine Serie mit zwei Fotografien ihre Gültigkeit haben kann. Viele Fotografien sind auch als Einzelbild aussagekräftig, gewinnen aber durch die übrigen Bilder der jeweiligen Serie an Gehalt. Manche brauchen geradezu die Alleinstellung, um zwischen zwei Serien voll zur Wirkung zu kommen. Diese Kraft der Bilder wurde bei der begrenzten Auswahl für das Buch berücksichtigt.

Allen Serien von Innenräumen in diesem Projekt ist gemein, dass deren Einzelfotografien nie von dem gleichen Aufnahmestandort aus gemacht wurden. Selbst wenn es sich um drei Ansichten desselben Raumes handelt, hat sich Rosswog jeweils den für ihn einzig möglichen neuen Punkt gesucht. Dabei geht er gerade bei kleineren Räumen sehr eng an die Raumwand, um möglichst viel vom Interieur einfangen zu können. Das leichte Weitwinkelobjektiv kommt seinem Bestreben dabei entgegen. Seine Außenaufnahmen können dagegen Panoramacharakter bekommen – dieser Effekt korrespondiert mit der Erfassung der landschaftlichen Einbettung der Hofanlagen. Nur bei diesen Außenaufnahmen kommt sowohl Schwarzweiß- als auch Farbnegativ-Material zum Einsatz. Die Interieurs sind stets in Farbe, die Porträts immer in Schwarzweiß gehalten. Wie die Bechers versucht auch Rosswog, bei seinen Außenaufnahmen eine »größtmögliche Schattenfreiheit« durch lange Belichtungszeiten und diffuses Licht zu erzielen.[10] Eine wilde Wolkenlandschaft wird man bei ihm vergeblich suchen. Soweit man bei Rosswog von bildlichen Typen sprechen kann, sind sie eher durch verschiedene Raumfunktionen definiert: Wohnen, Kochen, Bügeln, Schreiben, Schlafen, Baden, Lagern, Abstellen.

Gemeinsam ist unserem Projekt die Region Münsterland. Aus dem unterschiedlichen Alter der Bewohner und den wechselnden Familienkonstellationen ergaben sich die Anlässe und Zeitpunkte, zu denen in der Vergangenheit Veränderungen oder Erneuerungen der Einrichtung vorgenommen wurden. Ein häufiger Anlass für Neugestaltungen waren Hochzeiten und die damit verbundenen Generationswechsel – wie es auch andernorts zu beobachten ist. Anders als bei seinen Reisen in die Randregionen Europas, auf denen Rosswog allein lebende ältere Menschen gesucht und gefunden hat, hatten wir es im Münsterland mit mehr oder weniger großen Familien zu tun: Mutter und erwachsener Sohn, Eltern mit kleinen oder größeren Kindern oder auch drei Generationen unter einem Dach. Diese Familien ähneln unseren allgemeinen gesellschaftlichen Verhältnissen viel stärker, als es bei den Menschen in den anderen europäischen Ländern in Rosswogs Werk der Fall ist. Es fällt uns deshalb vielleicht hier auch leichter, Dinge aus unserem Lebenszusammenhang wiederzuentdecken. Es bleibt ein gewisses Staunen beim Betrachter nicht aus, wenn etwa das Bemühen der Bewohner um eine eigene Ästhetik zu erkennen ist. Hier spielt das Bedürfnis nach Symmetrie offenbar eine wichtige Rolle. Doch gerade die Kombination von Alt und Neu, von wertvollen Antiquitäten und Möbeln aus dem Einrichtungshaus, von Aufgeräumtheit und Unordnung dicht beieinander, macht den Alltag, das »pralle Leben« sichtbar.

Dieser intime Einblick in das aktuelle Leben beschäftigt nicht nur Kulturwissenschaftler, auch in der aktuellen Fotoszene gibt es Parallelen oder gar Nachfolger. Inzwischen ist zum Beispiel unter dem Label »Helsinki School« eine junge Fotografengeneration in Finnland und nicht nur dort zu beachtlicher Anerkennung gelangt.[11] Sie orientiert sich, wie sie selbst bekundet, an der Becherschen Schule. Hat sie vielleicht Martin Rosswogs Werk im Blick und wird sie zukünftig ebenfalls stärker seriell arbeiten? Rosswogs Bilder waren jedenfalls 1997 in Helsinki und Tampere zu sehen. Diese spannenden Entwicklungen bleiben zu beobachten.

»inside houses«

Für dieses Buch und die Detmolder Ausstellung *»inside* – Schultenhöfe des Münsterlandes« hat der Künstler wichtige Fotografien aus dem Gesamtprojekt ausgewählt und zusammengestellt.[12] Lassen Sie sich von diesen Fotografien direkt ansprechen, sie machen süchtig. Es ist eine Seh-Sucht, die sich einstellt, sofern man sich auf das Experiment einlässt, für eine Zeit die Sehweise des Künstlers anzunehmen. Wer die Bilder genau betrachtet, sieht die Dinge des Alltags mit anderen Augen. So dokumentiert Martin Rosswog in seinen Aufnahmen die traditionelle Wohnkultur Europas in einer inhaltlichen und formalen Dichte, deren Wert besonders deutlich wird, wenn man sie mit den heute medial vermittelten Bildern vergleicht. Dies mag nicht zuletzt daran liegen, dass es sich bei seinen Fotografien um eine ideale Kombination aus Kunstwerk und Dokument handelt. Einmal in den Bann der Orte und Räume gezogen, möchte man andere auf diese Reise mitnehmen, die Türen öffnen – das ist das Anliegen dieses Buches und der Ausstellung. Nehmen Sie die *»inside«*-Perspektive ein – genau wie es der Ausstellungstitel verspricht – und haben Sie teil an einem Forschungsprojekt, das die Privatheit zur Ausgangsbasis für einen kreativen künstlerischen Schaffensprozess macht.

Anmerkungen

1 *Menschenbilder: Porträtfotografien von Martin Rosswog.* (Dumont Verlag) Köln 1989. Und ganz aktuell »Heritage – Fotografien von Martin Rosswog« im Rheinischen Landesmuseum Bonn, (Schirmer/Mosel) München 2005.

2 Leopold Schütte: »Schulte und Meier in (Nordost-)Westfalen«, in: *Spieker – Landeskundliche Beiträge und Berichte* 37, Münster 1995, S. 211–225.

3 Dem Team gehörte auch der Genealoge Jörg Wunschhofer (aus Beckum) an, dem an dieser Stelle herzlich gedankt sei.

4 Siehe Museumsführer: *Westfälisches Freilichtmuseum Detmold – Landesmuseum für Volkskunde.* Detmold 2001, S. 104–110, sowie Heinrich Stiewe: »Vom Umgang mit Häusern im Museum«, in: Stefan Baumeier und Jan Carstensen (Hrsg.): *Westfälisches Freilichtmuseum Detmold. Geschichte – Konzepte – Entwicklungen.* Detmold 1996, S. 69–108; hier S. 75ff.

5 Jan Carstensen, Thomas Düllo, Claudia Richartz-Sasse (Hrsg.): *ZimmerWelten – Wie junge Menschen heute wohnen. Schriften des Westfälischen Freilichtmuseums Detmold 23.* Essen 2000.

6 Andreas Graf: »Die Kunst erfinden und verbergen«, in: Martin Rosswog: *Inside Houses. Rural Homes in Europe/Ländliches Wohnen in Europa/Maisons rustique en Europe.* Köln 2001, S. XI–XVIII, hier S. XI.

7 Graf 2001 (wie Anm. 6), S. XVII.

8 Martina Dobbe: *Bernd und Hilla Becher, Fachwerkhäuser.* Museum der Gegenwartskunst Siegen, Schriftenreihe Bd. 1, Siegen 2001.

9 Dobbe 2001 (wie Anm. 8), S. 29.

10 Dobbe 2001 (wie Anm. 8), S. 42.

11 *The Helsinki School. Photography by TaiK, issued by the University of Art and Design Helsinki.* Ostfildern 2005.

12 Für das Projekt »Schultenhöfe« ist eine Gesamtdokumentation mit rund 500 Aufnahmen in Schwarzweiß und in Farbe entstanden. Davon konnten über 150 Fotografien vom Westfälischen Freilichtmuseum Detmold angekauft werden. Die Schwarzweiß-Fotografien haben das Format ca. 27 x 38 cm, die Farbfotografien ca. 22 x 30 cm.

Tafeln / Plates

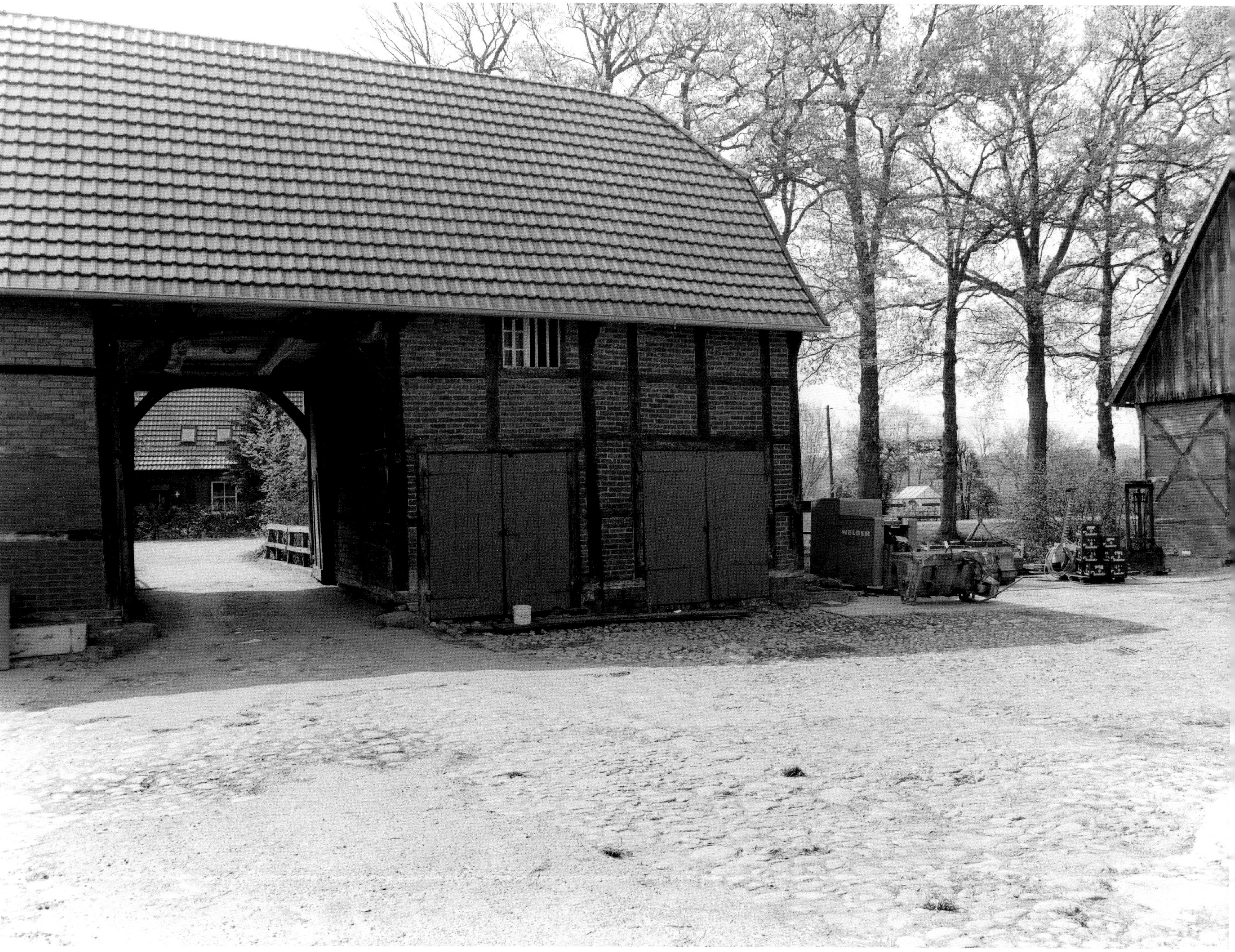
WELGER

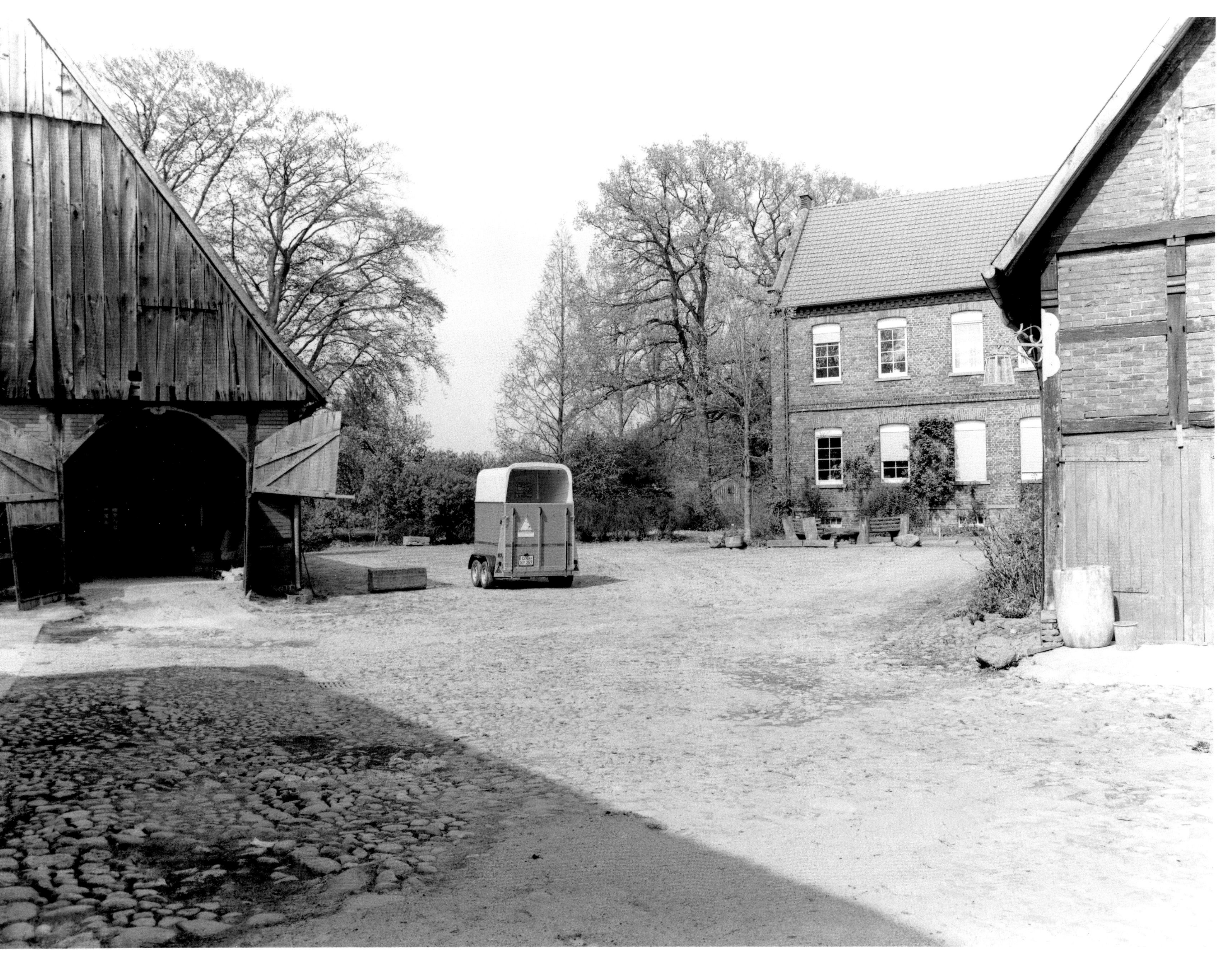

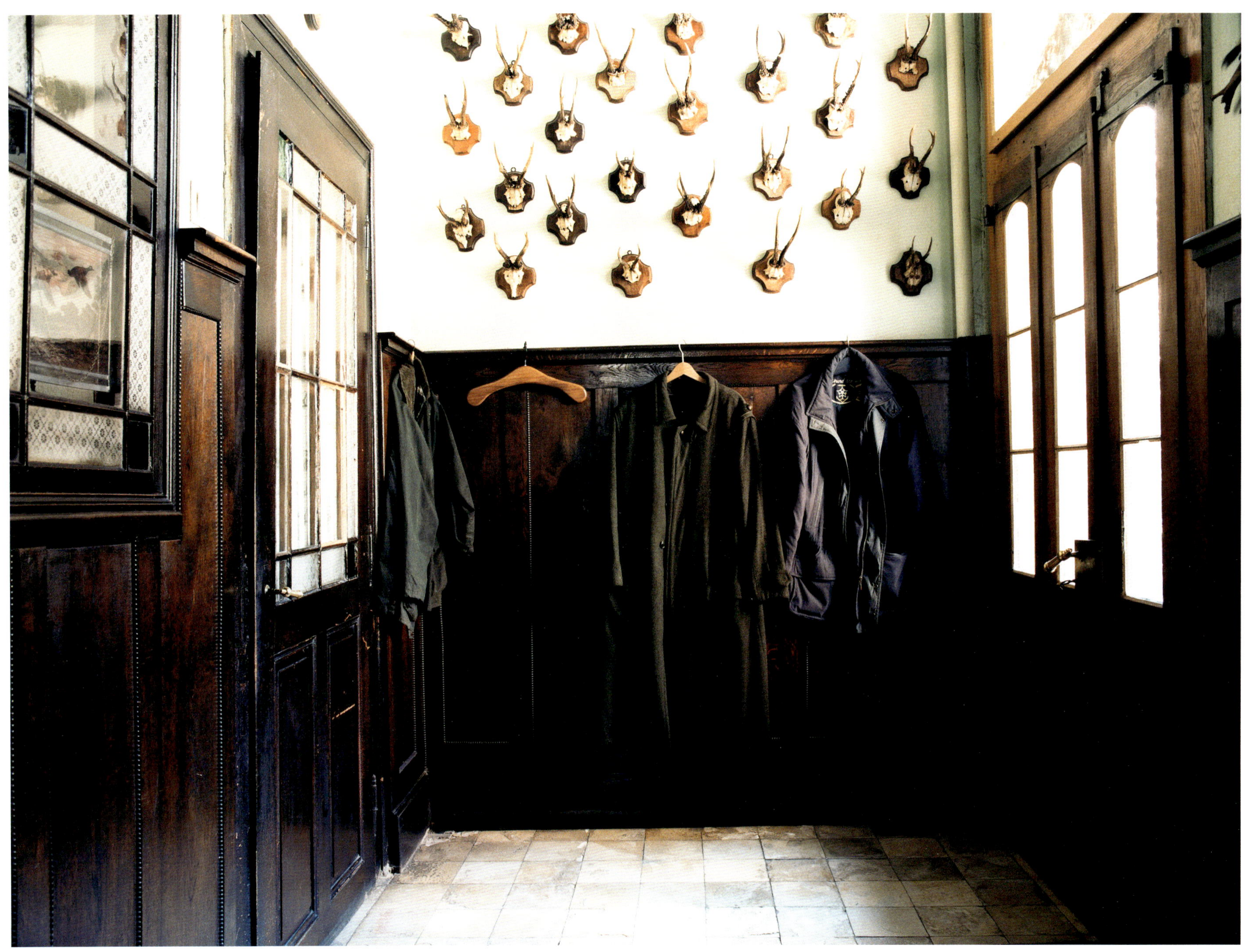

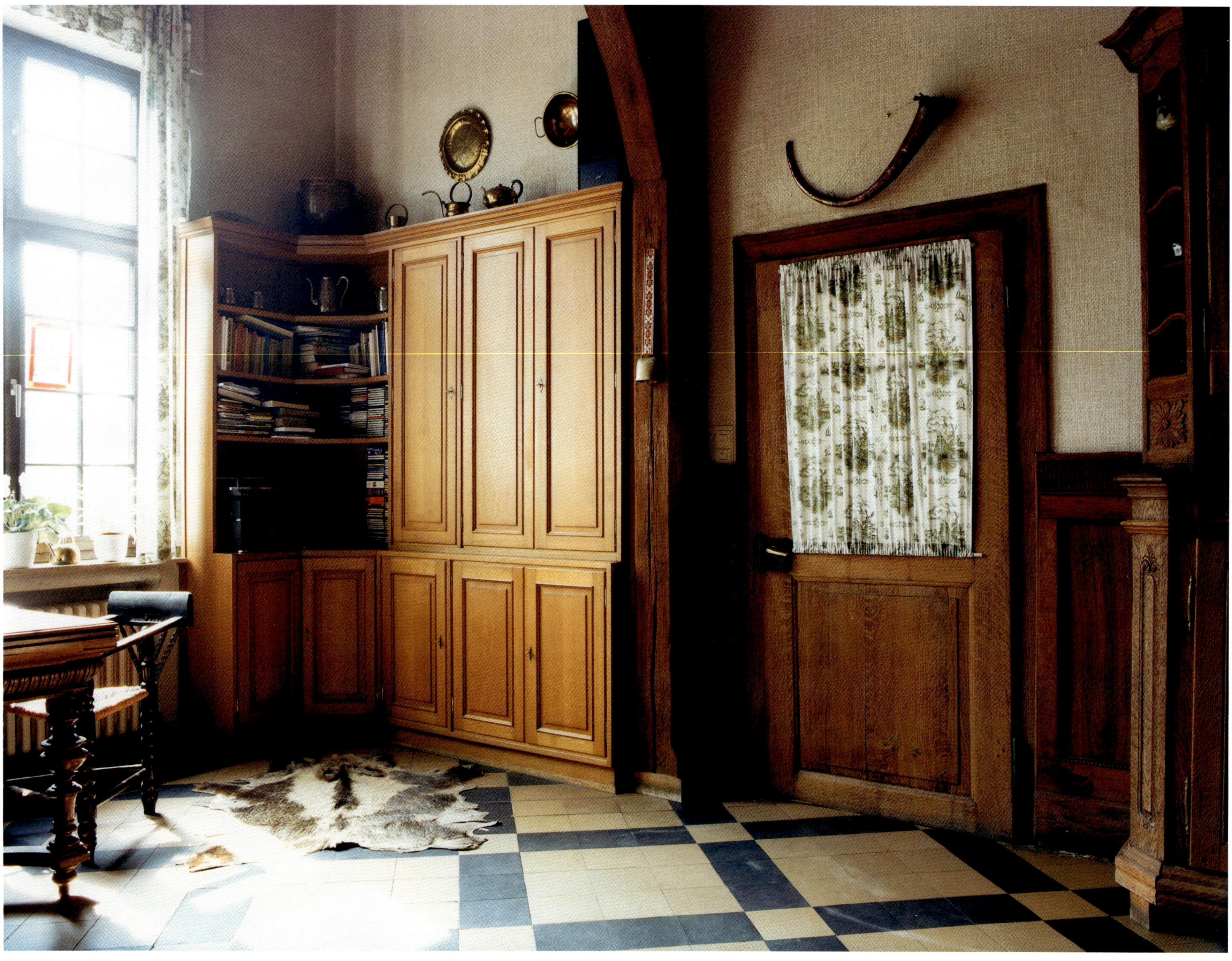

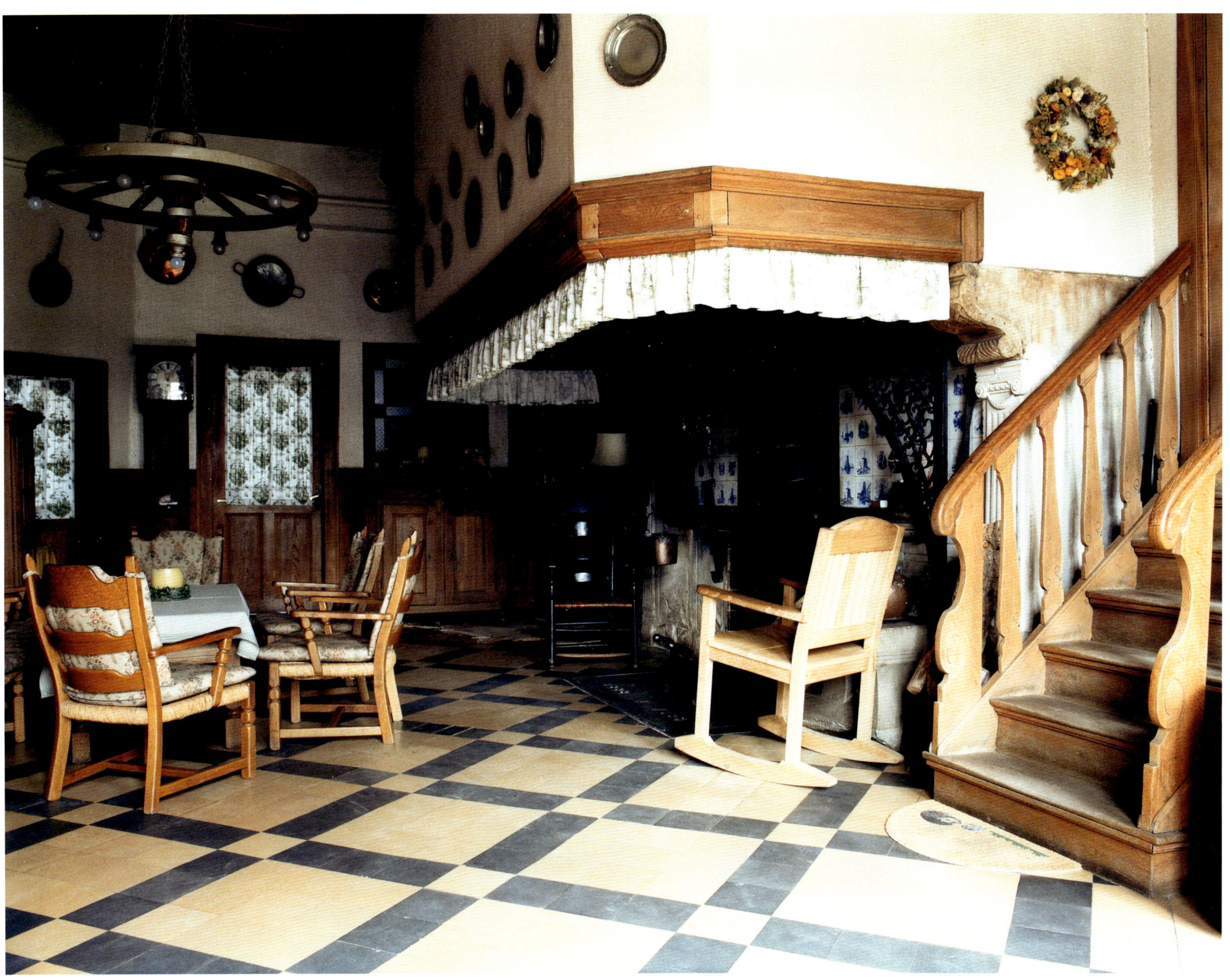

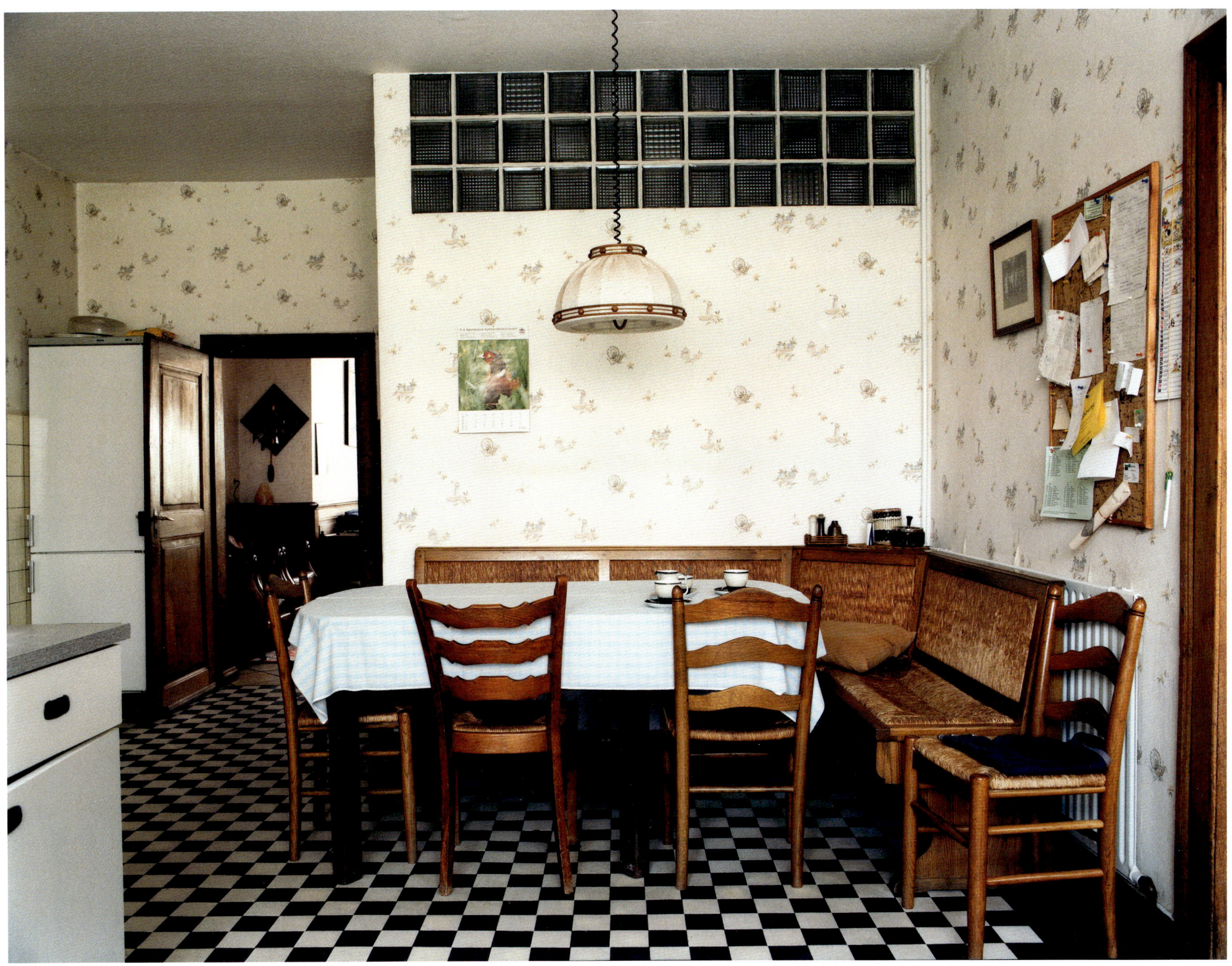

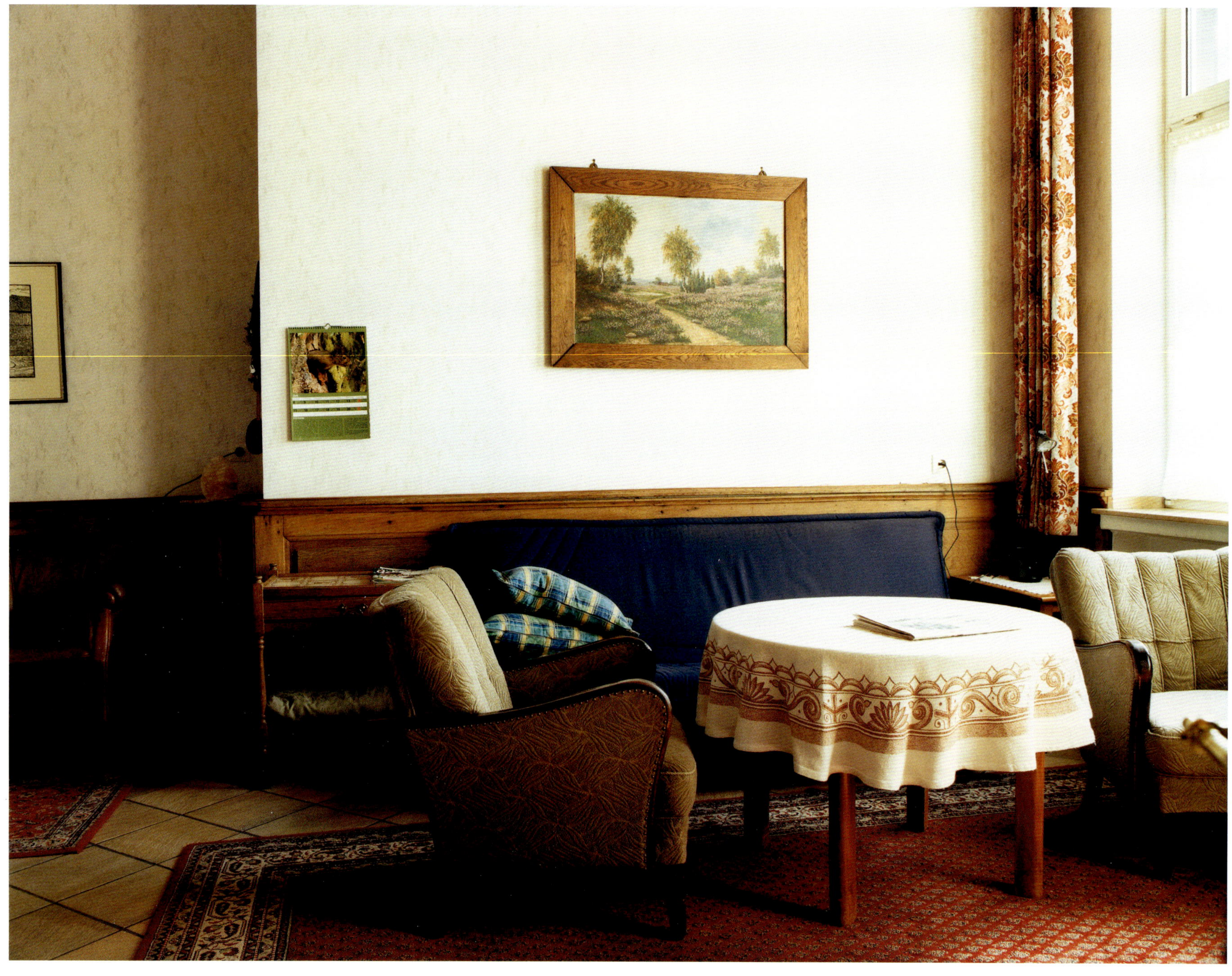

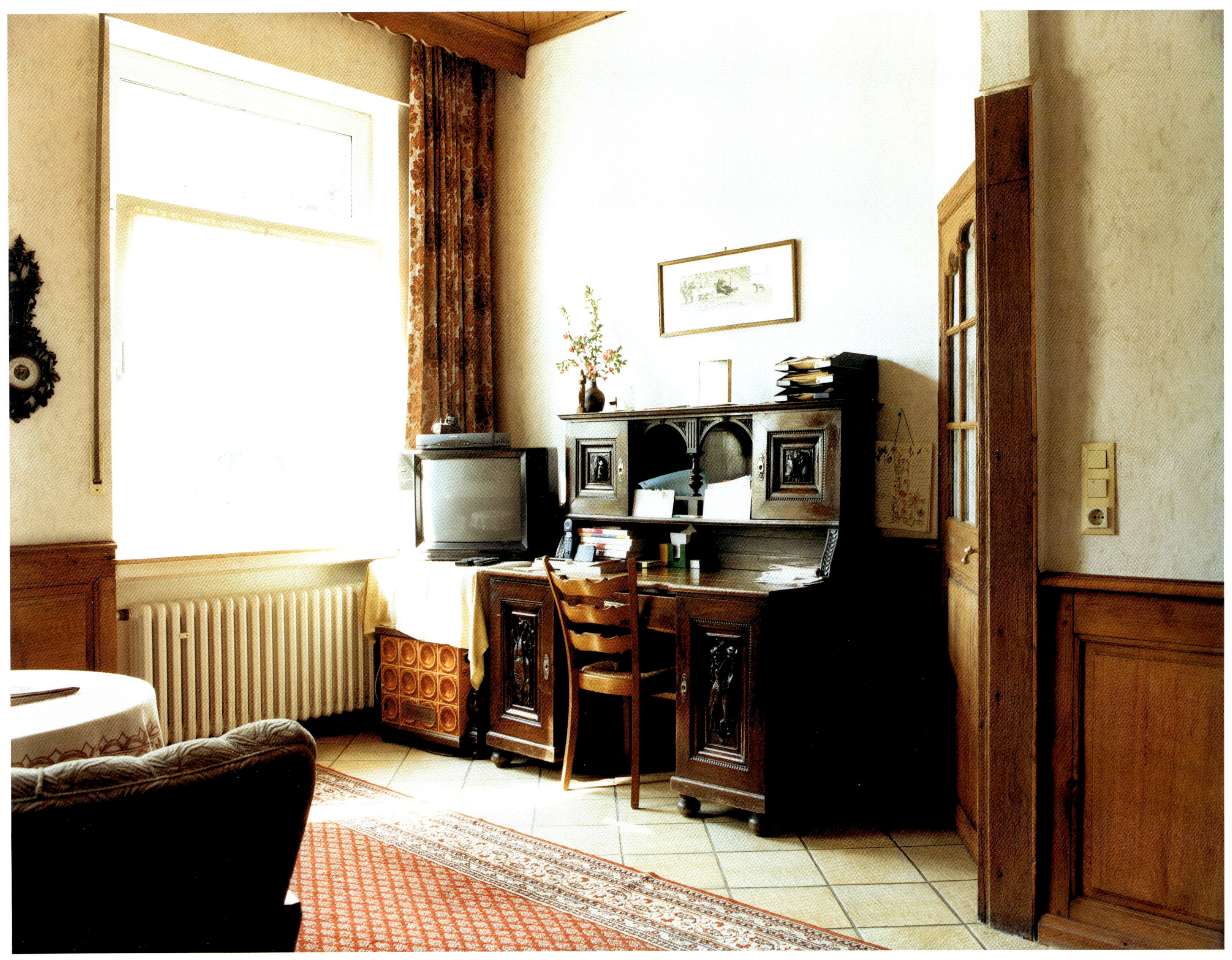

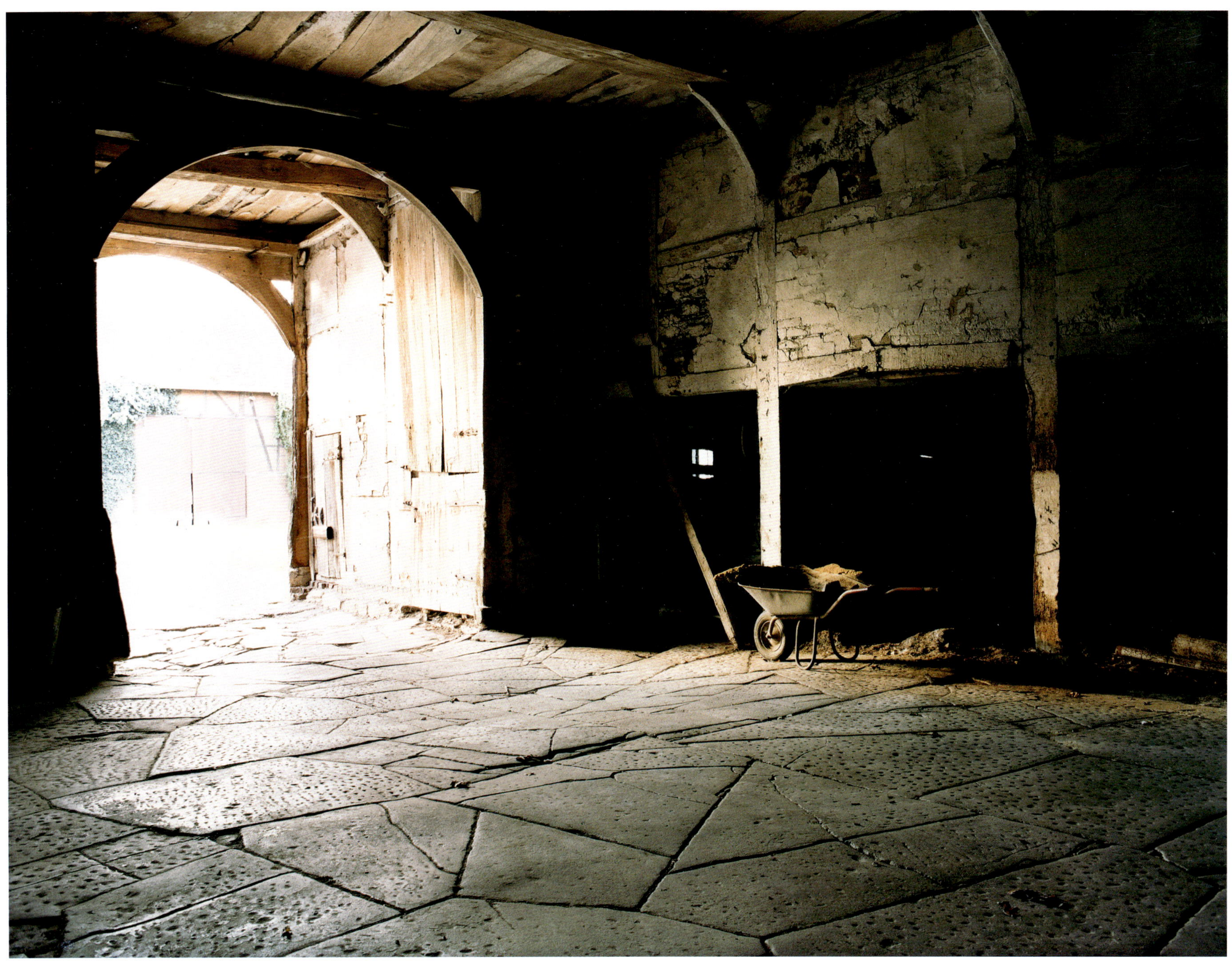

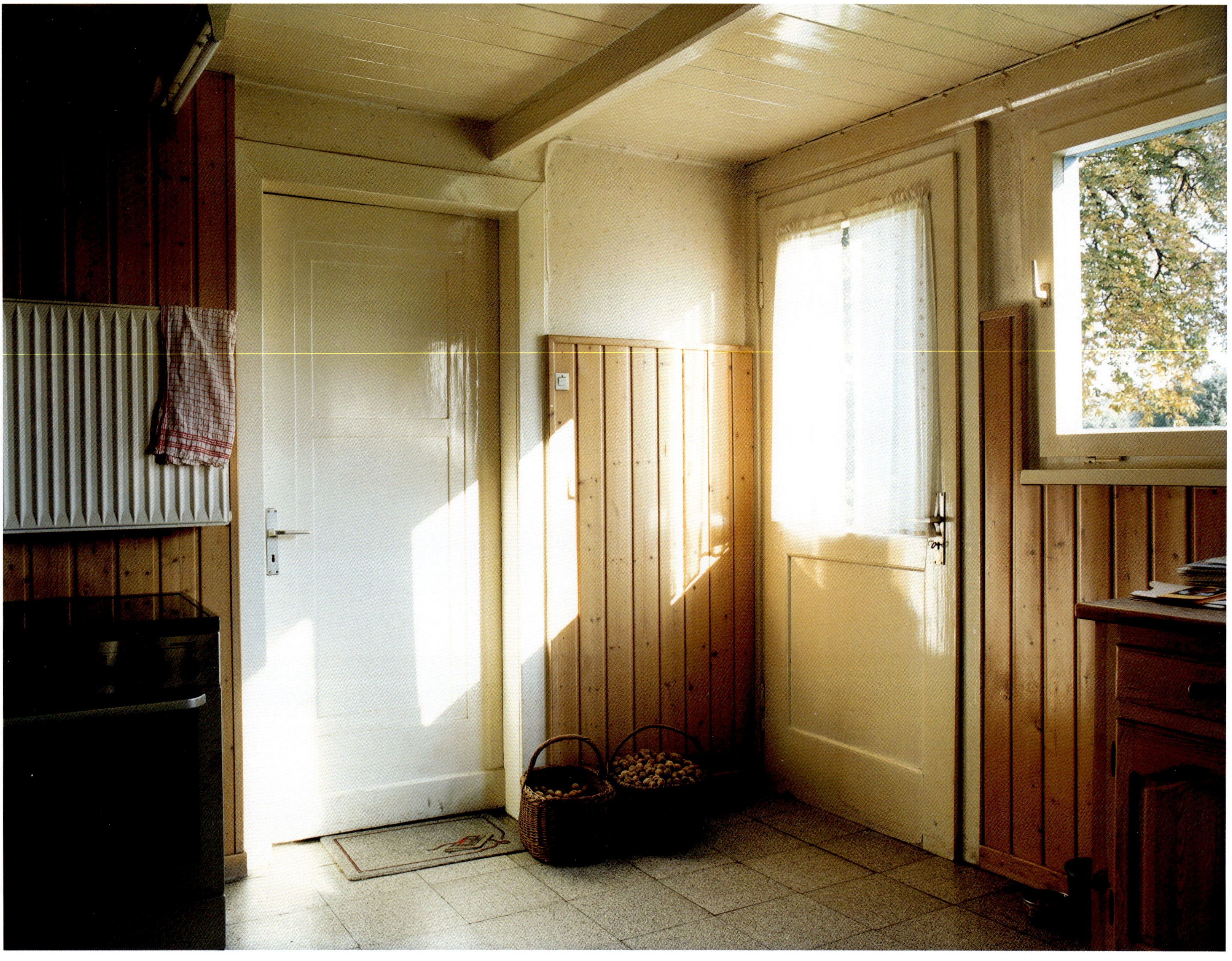

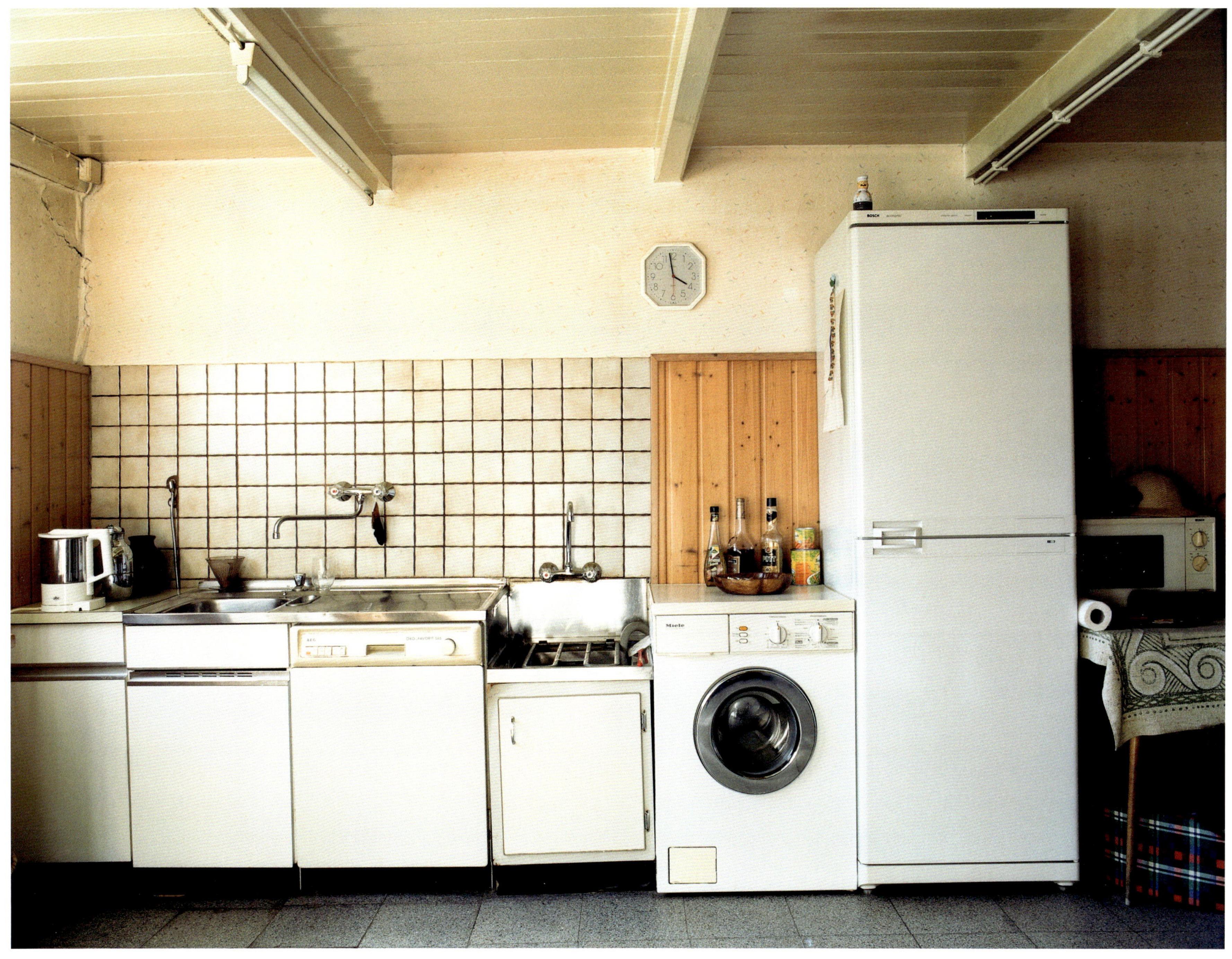

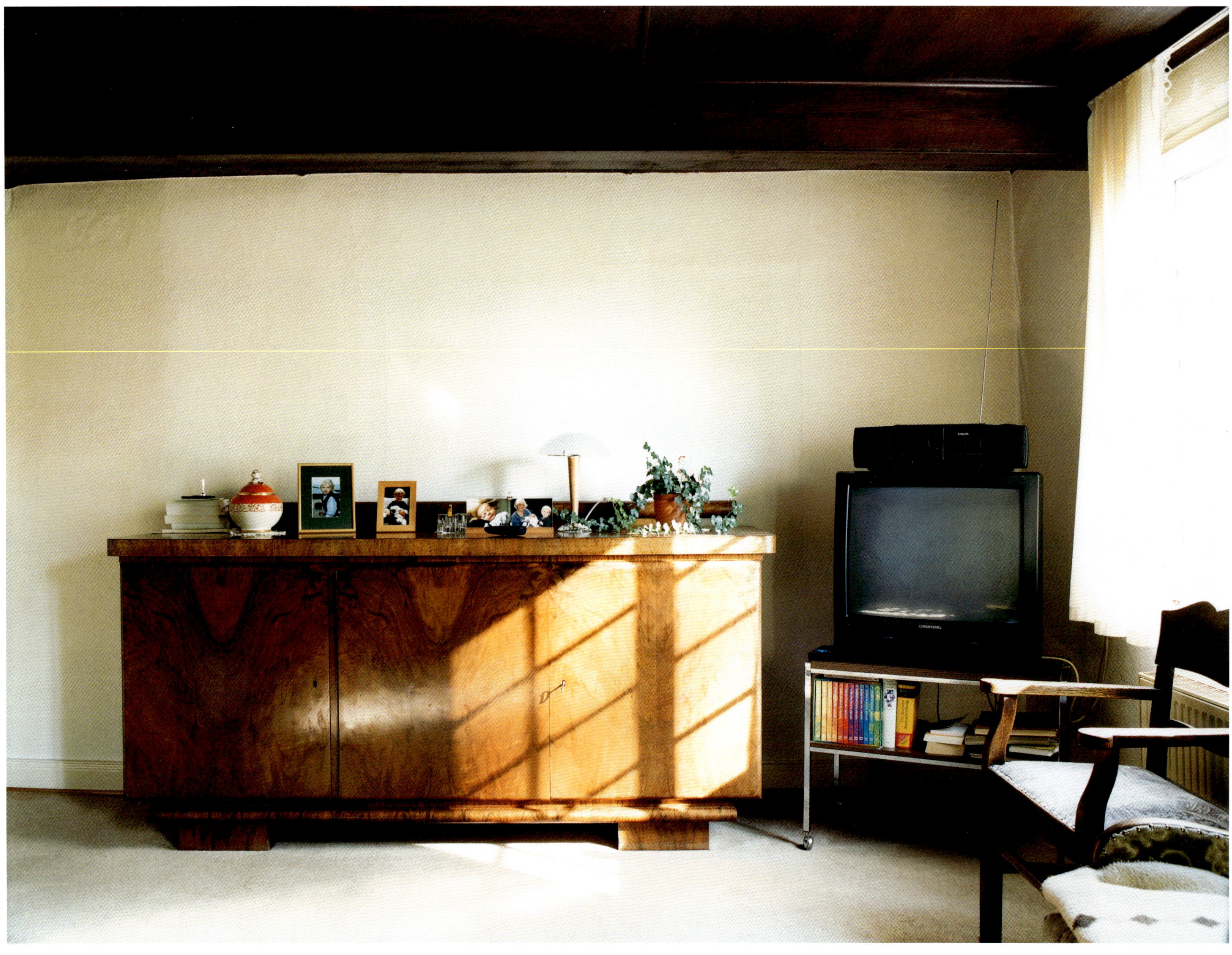

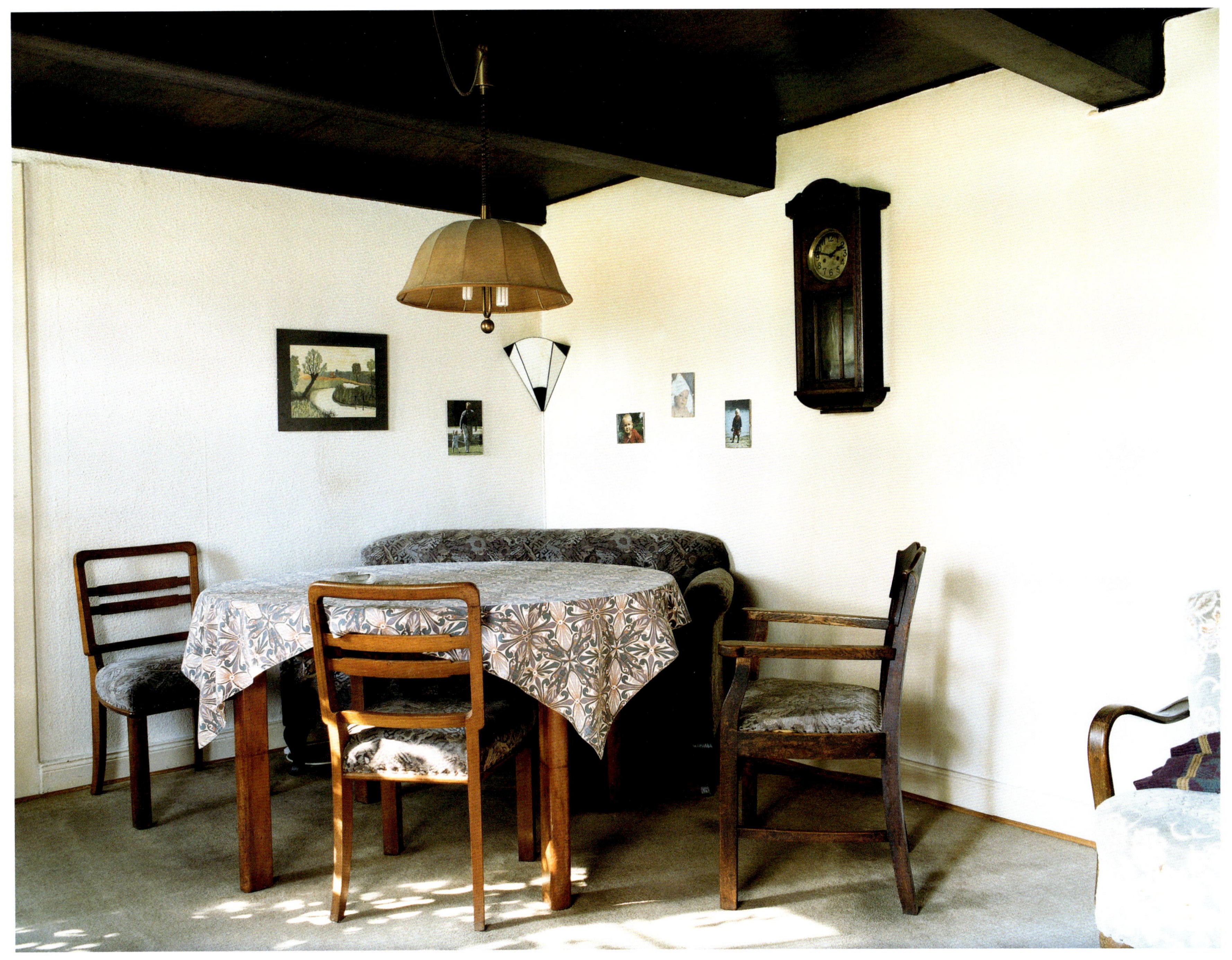

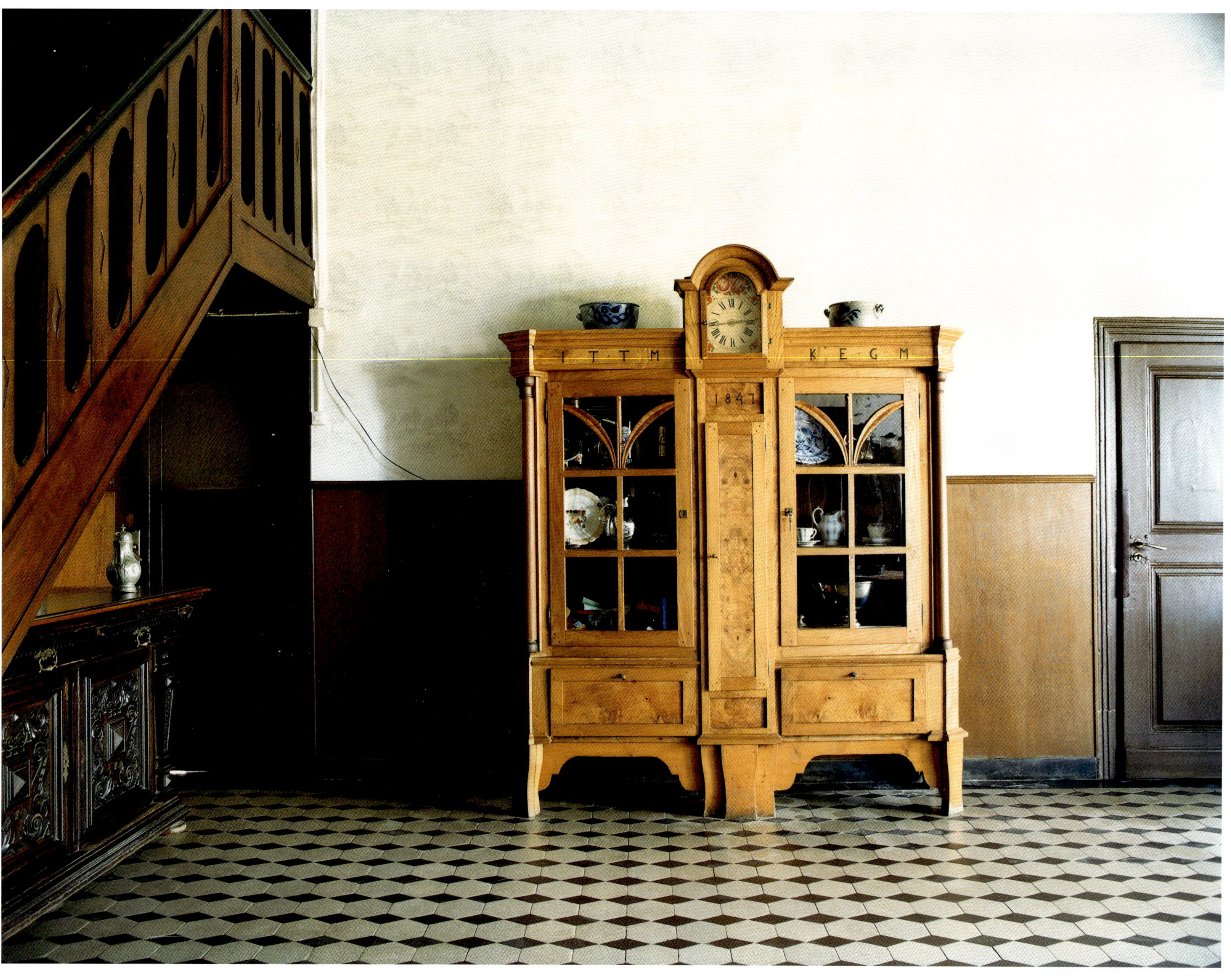
I T T M
K E G M
1847

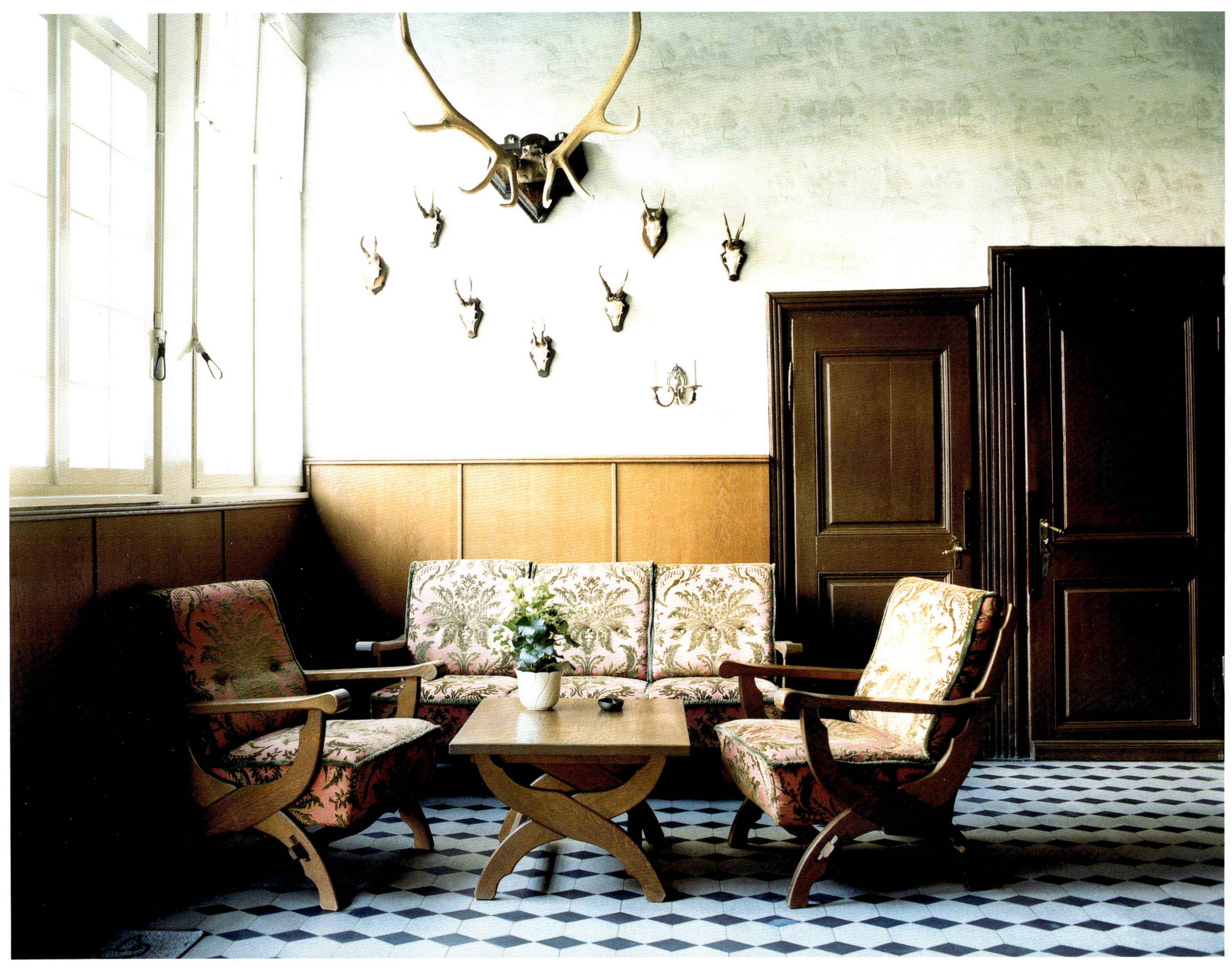

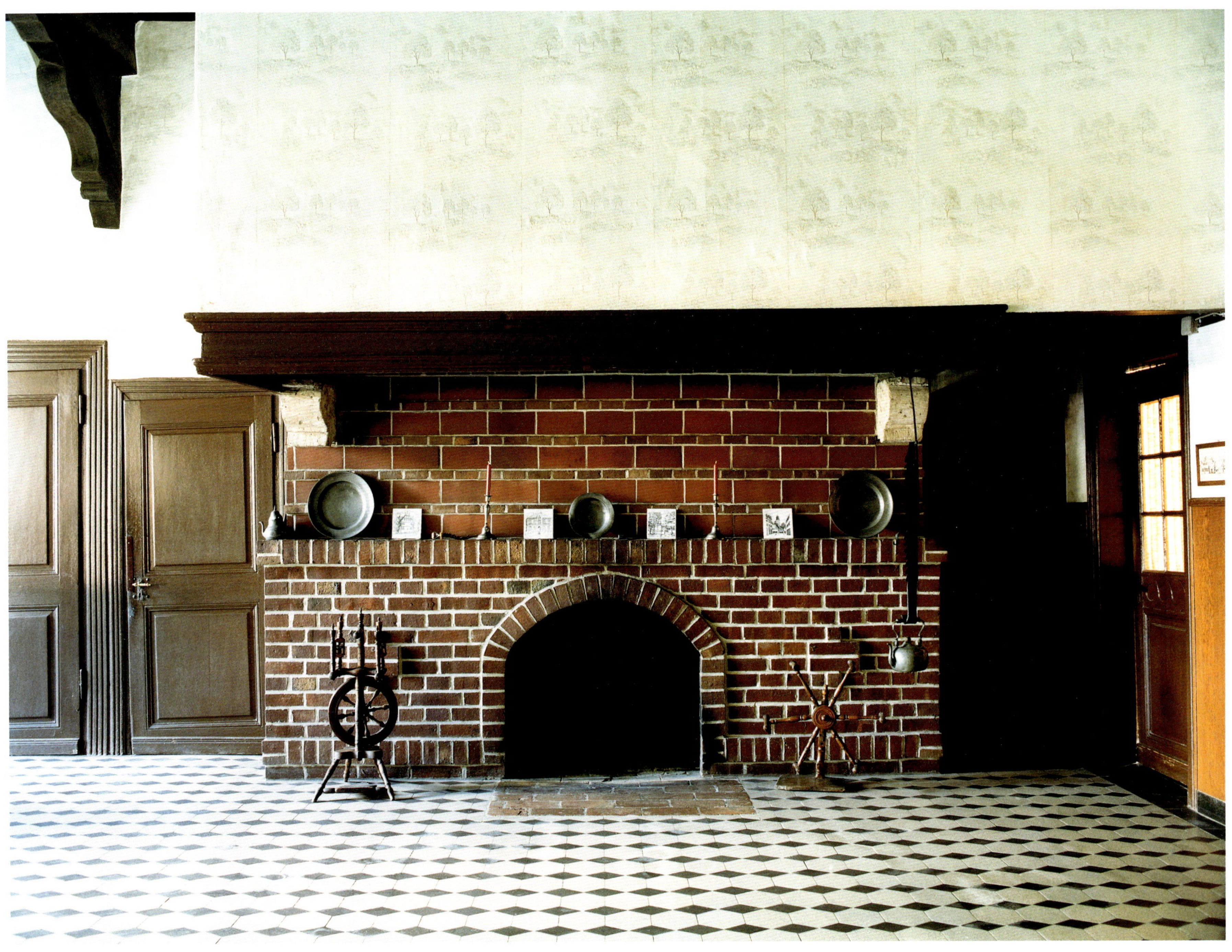

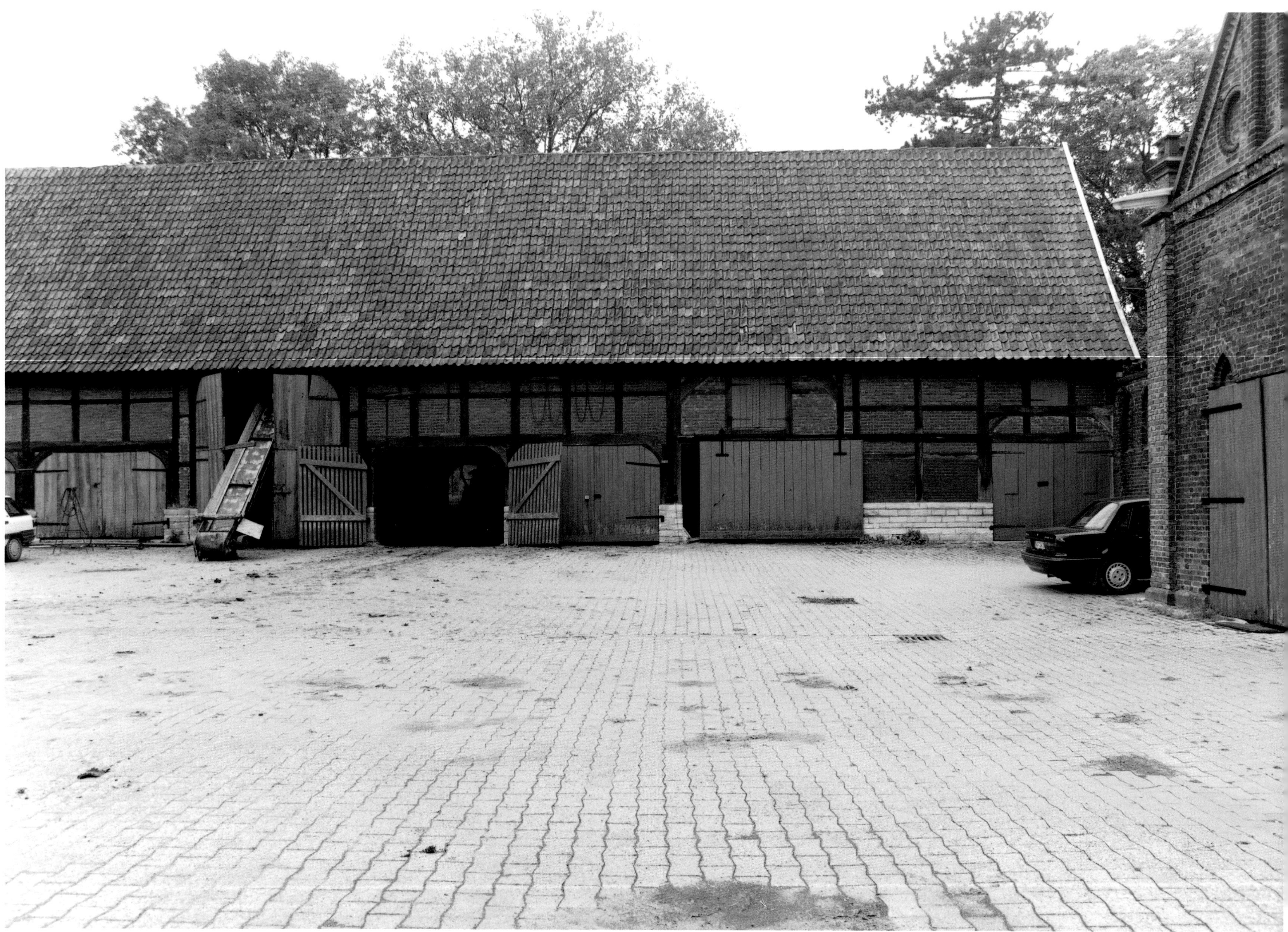

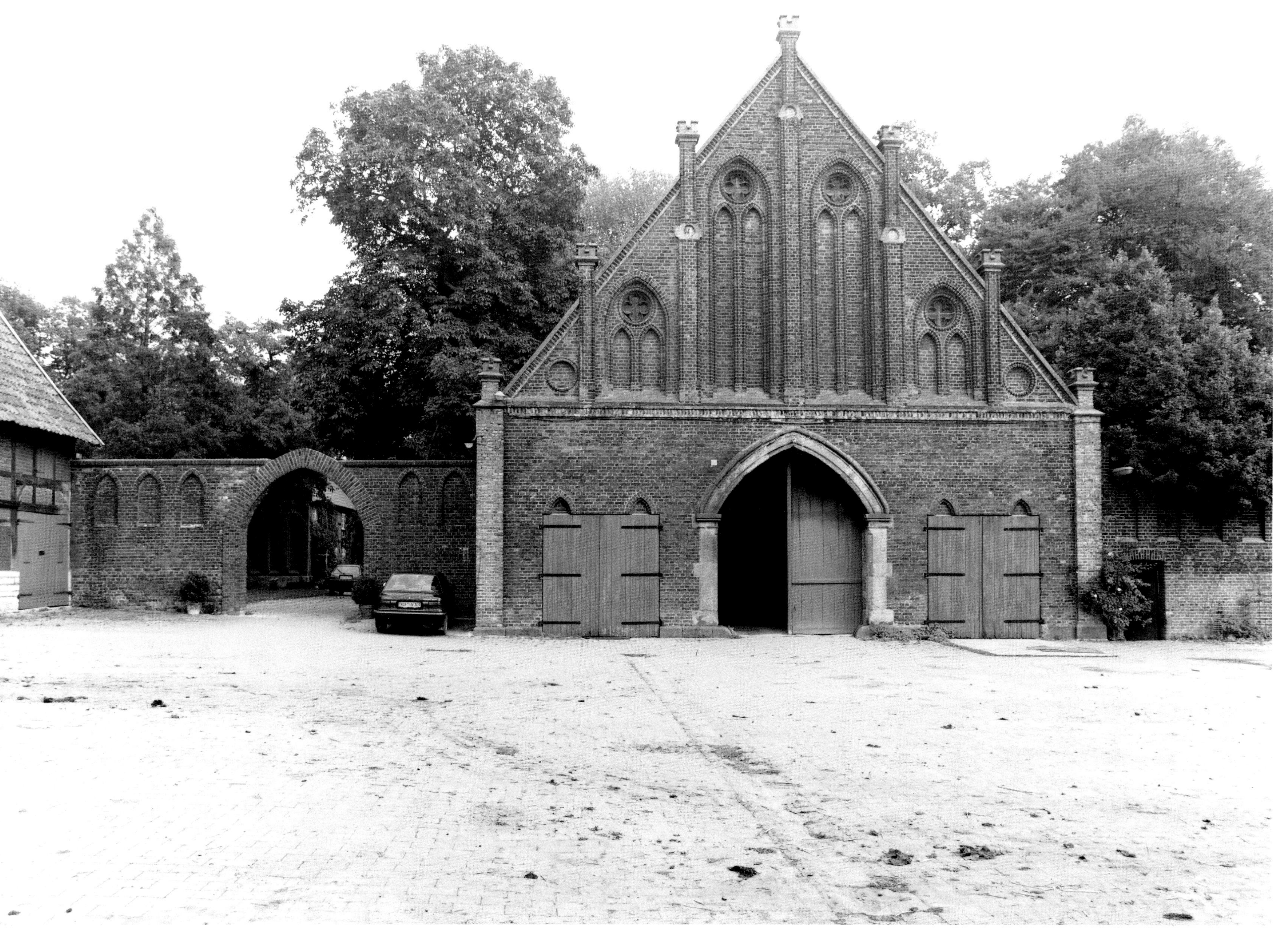

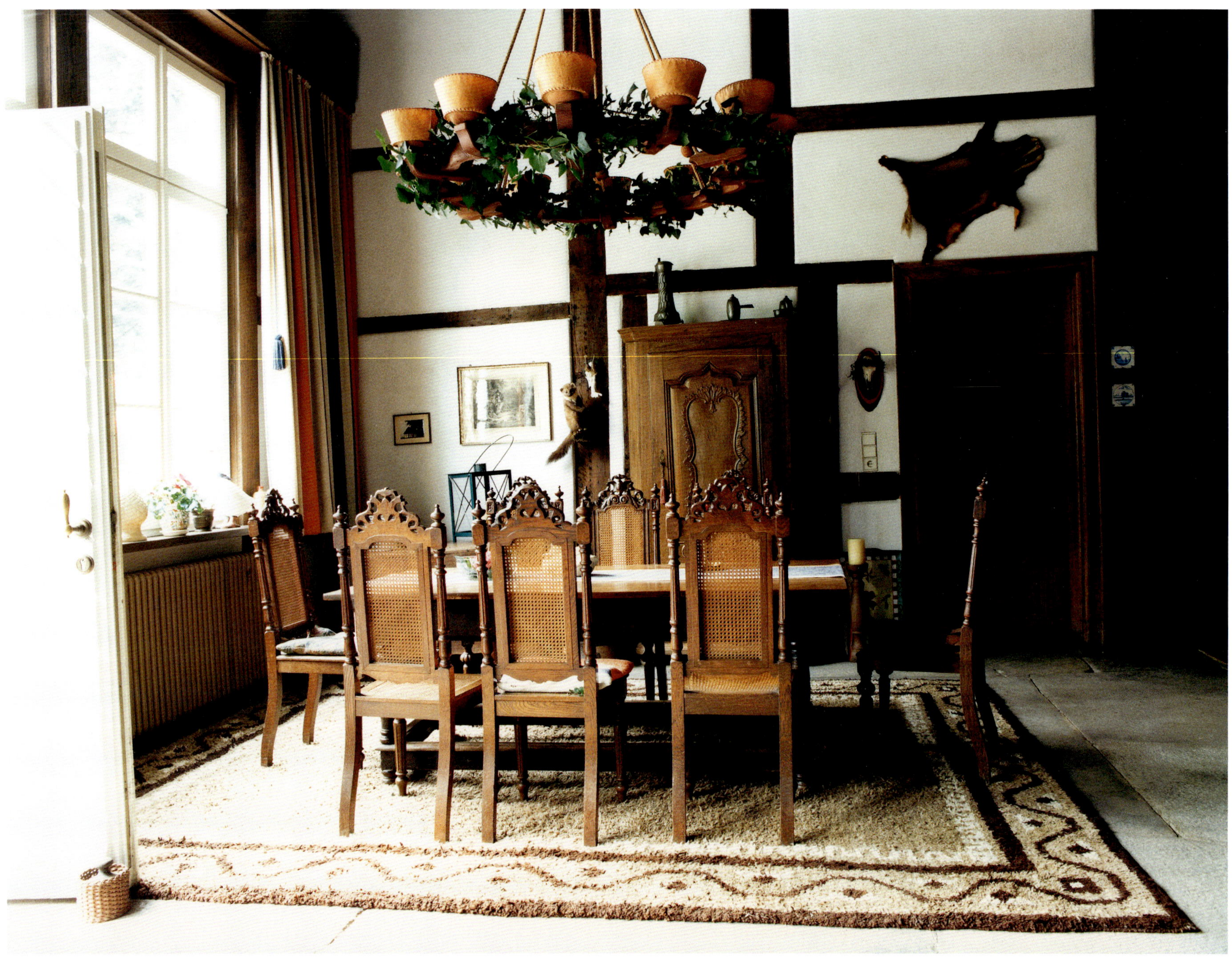

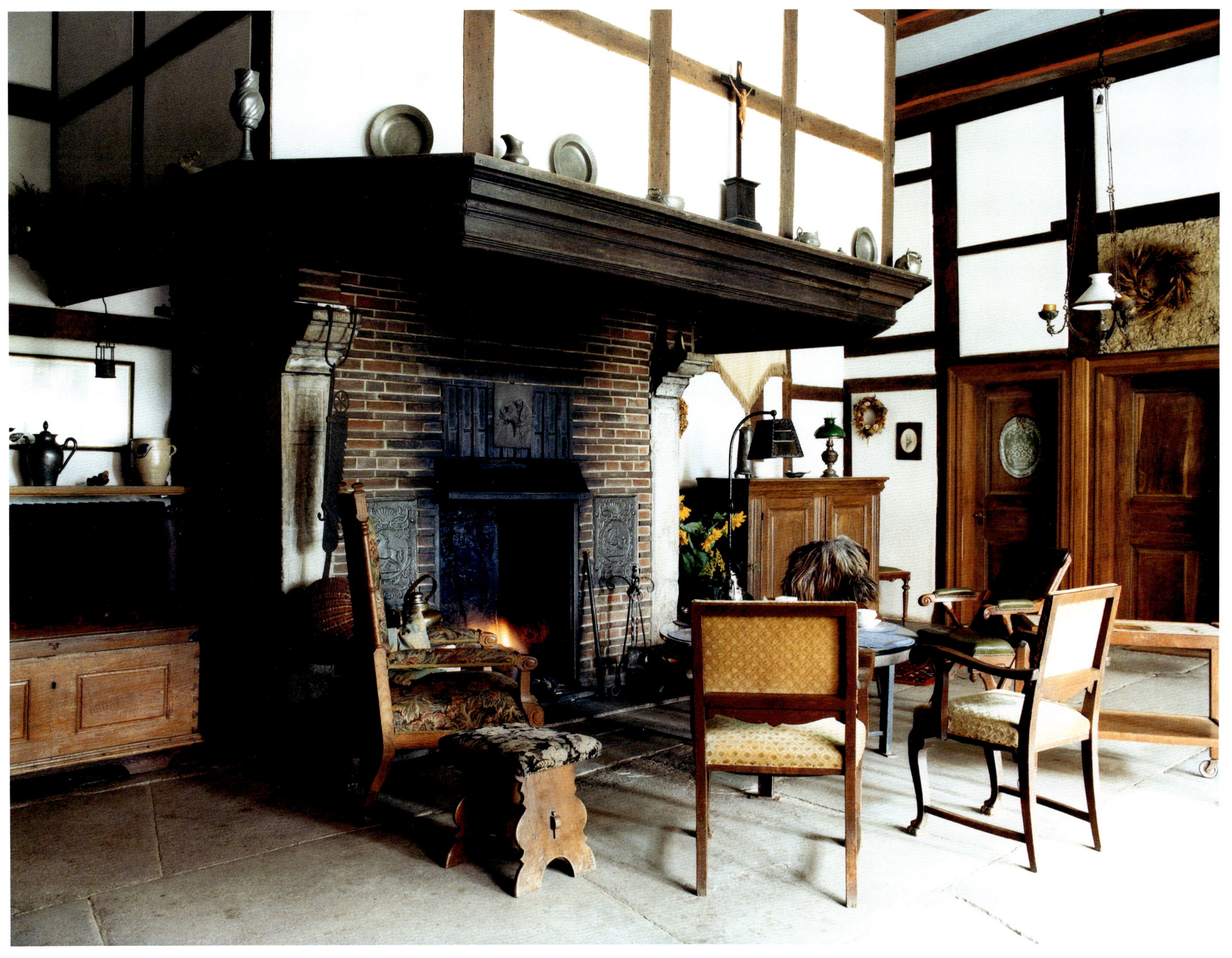

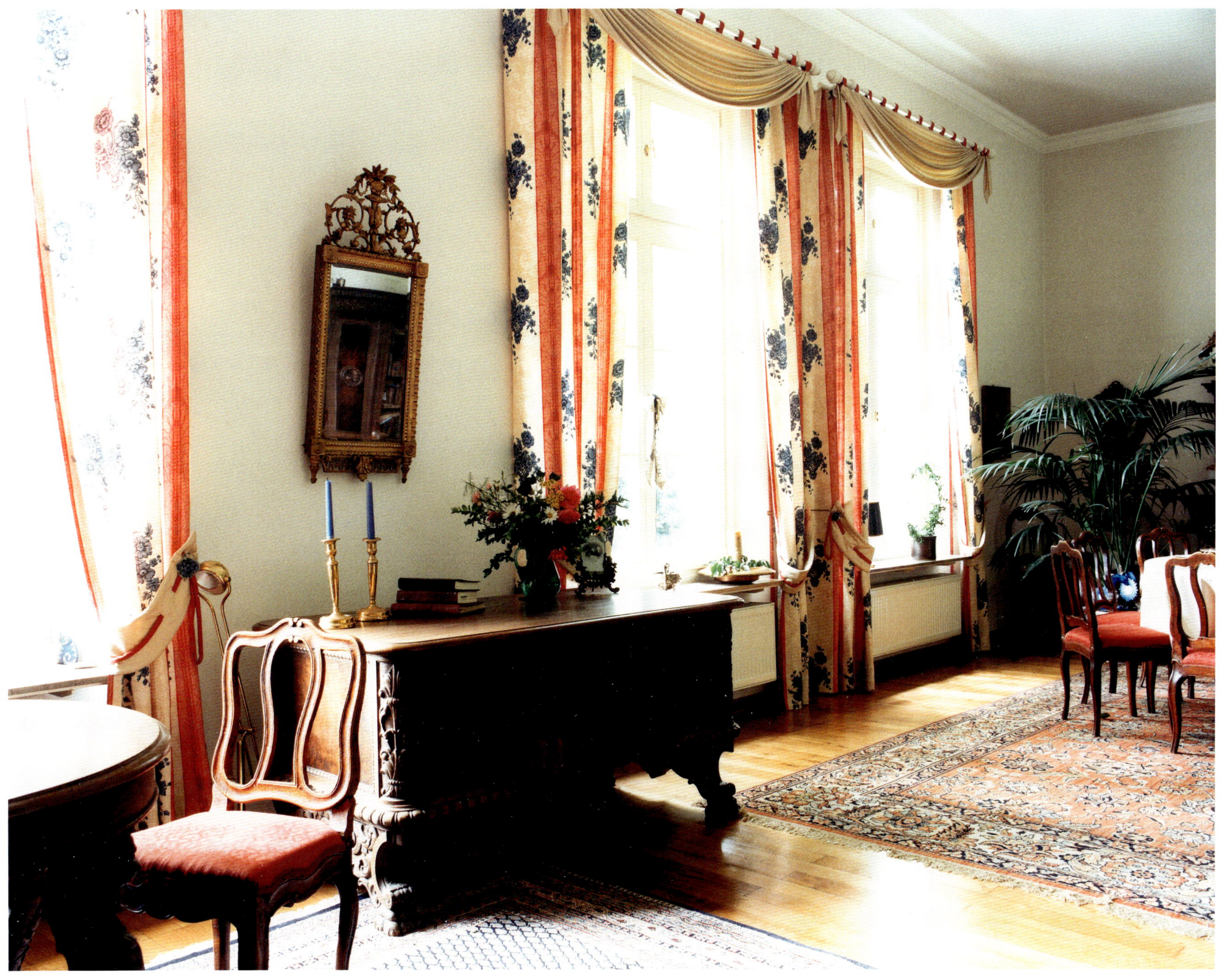

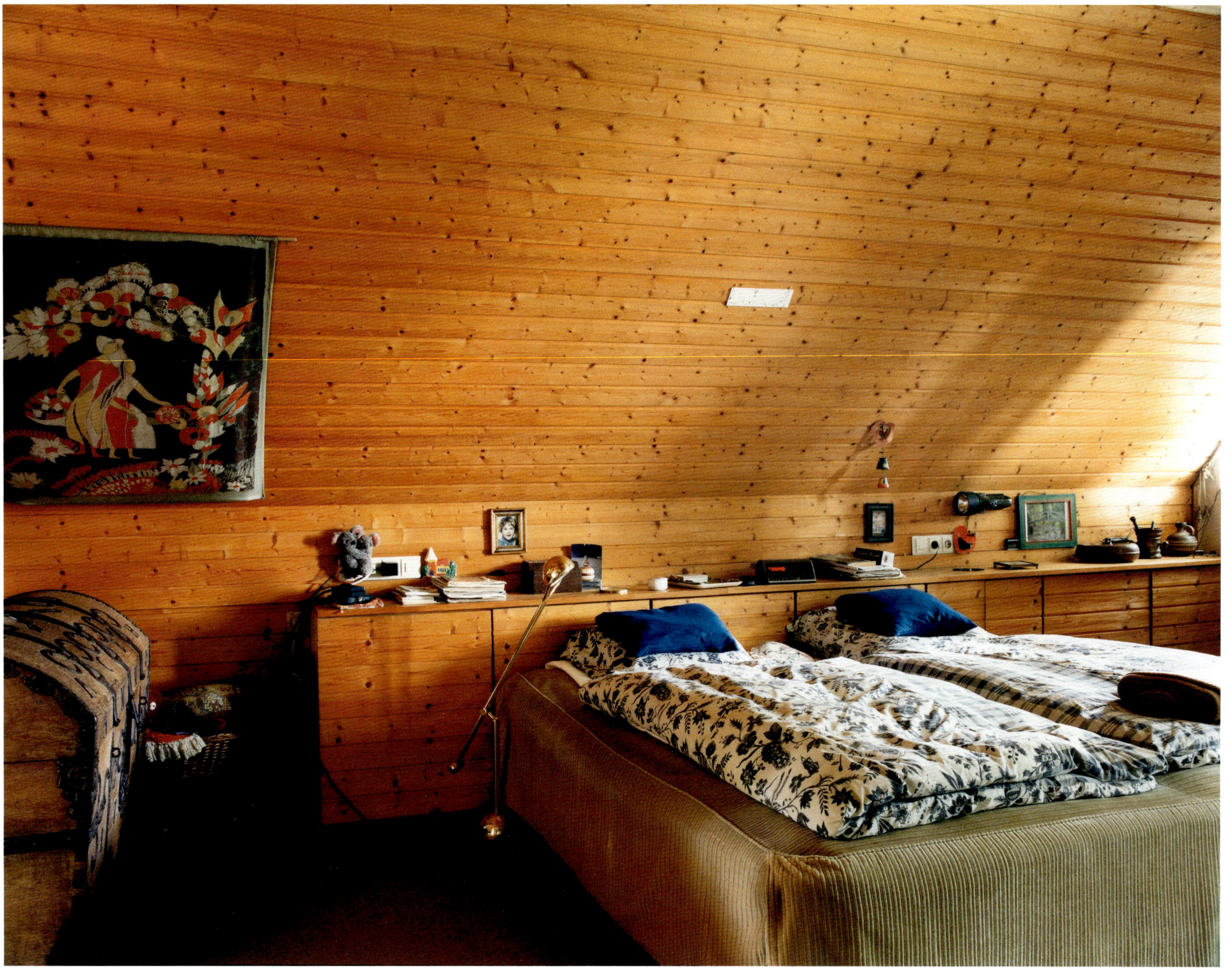

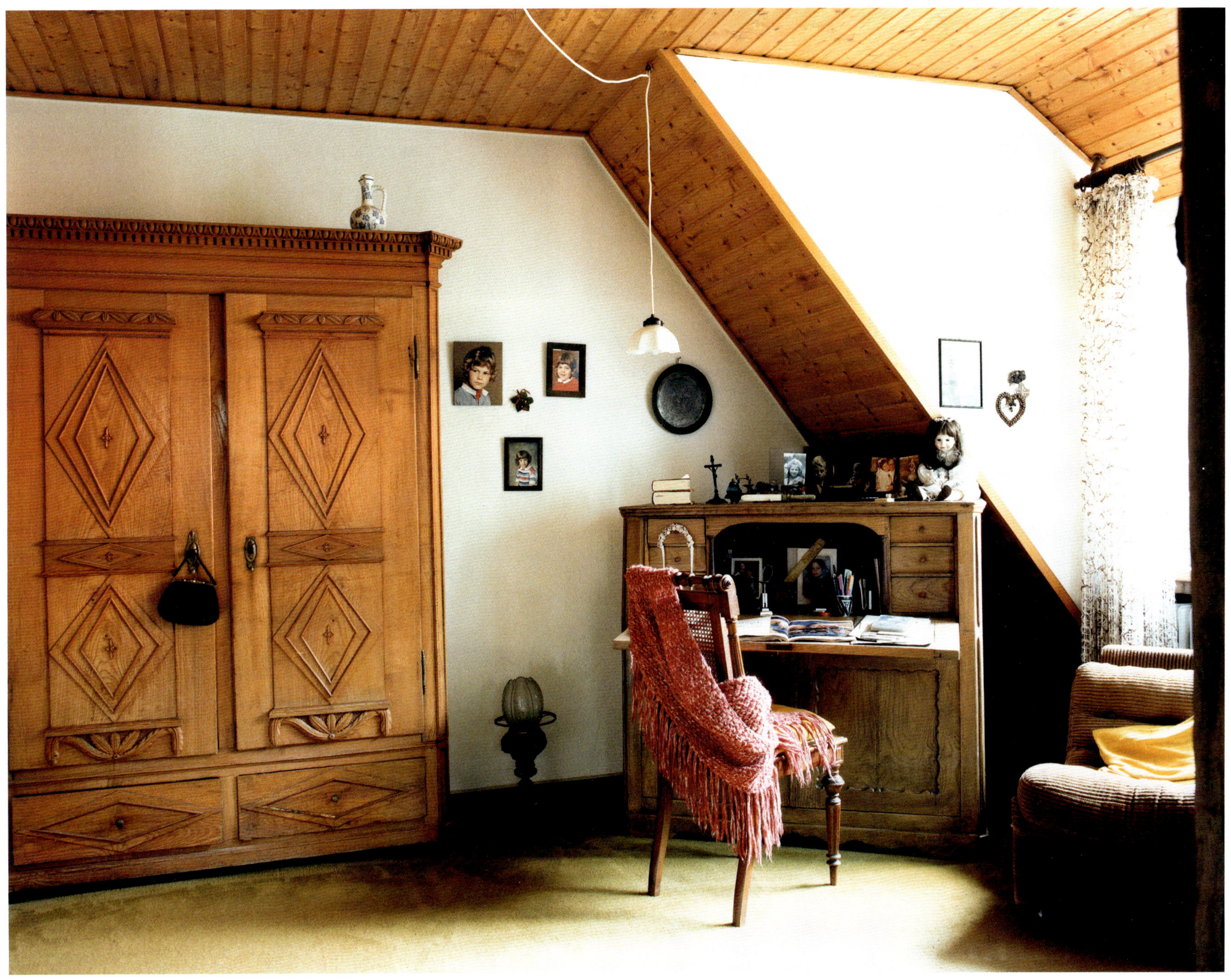

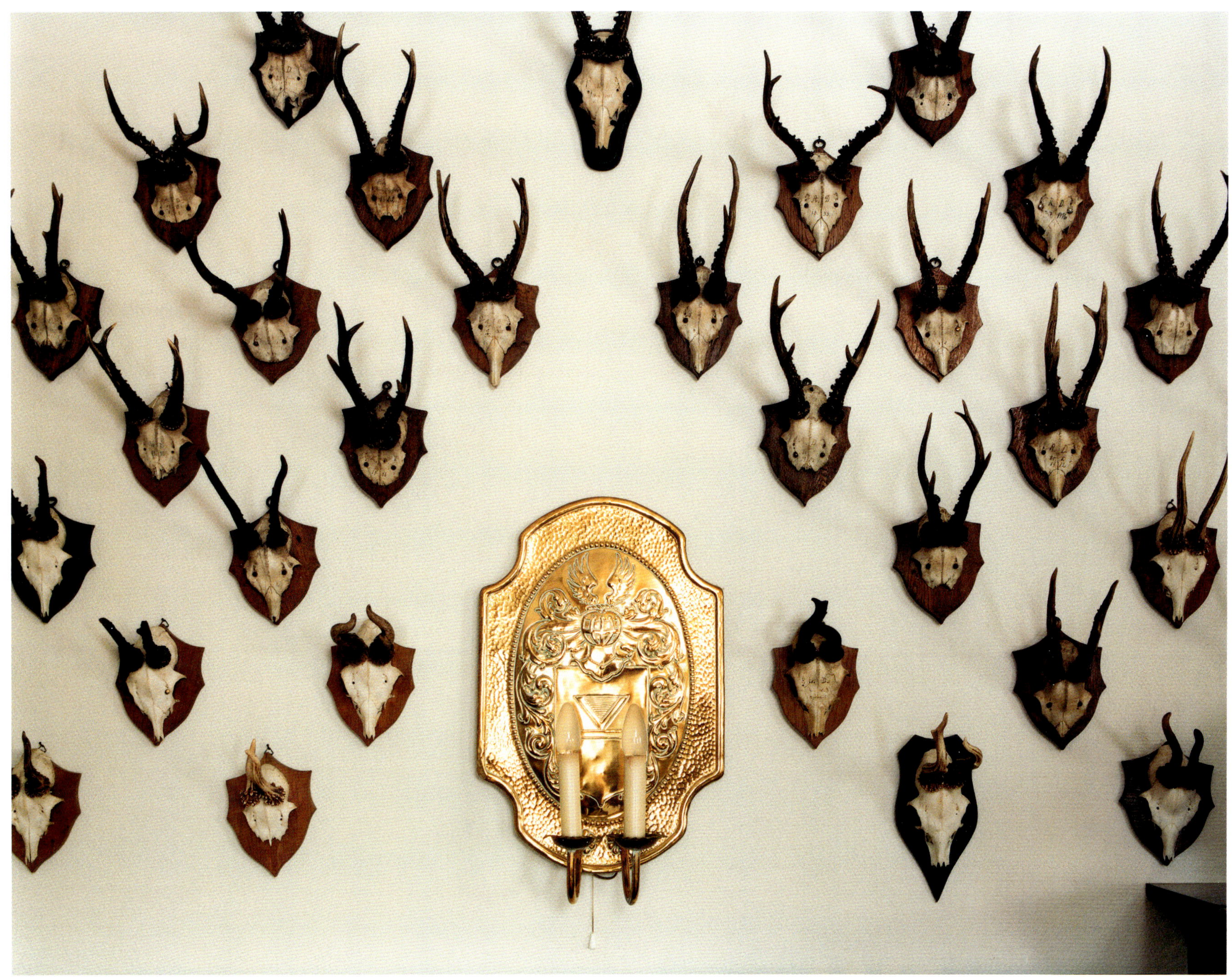

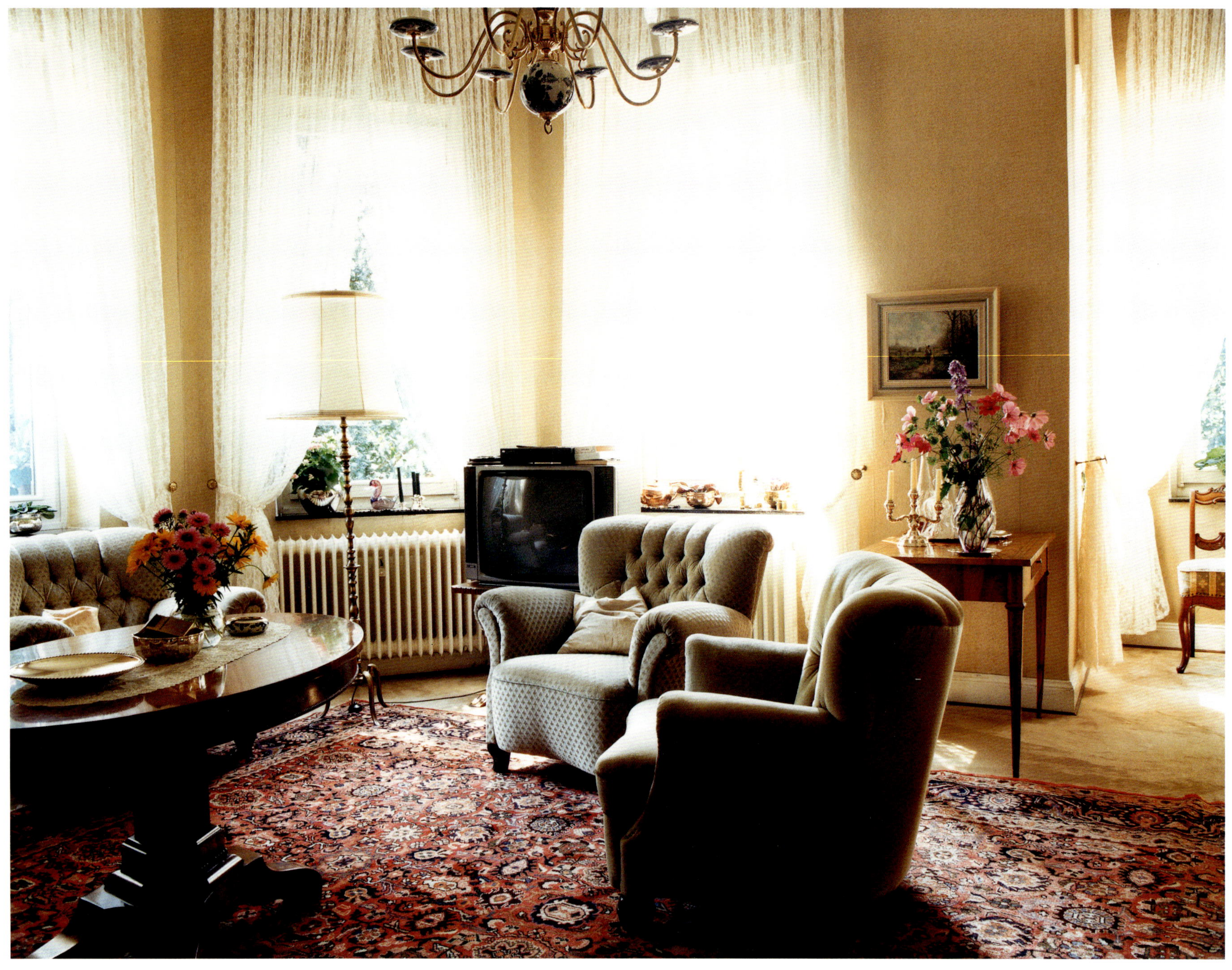

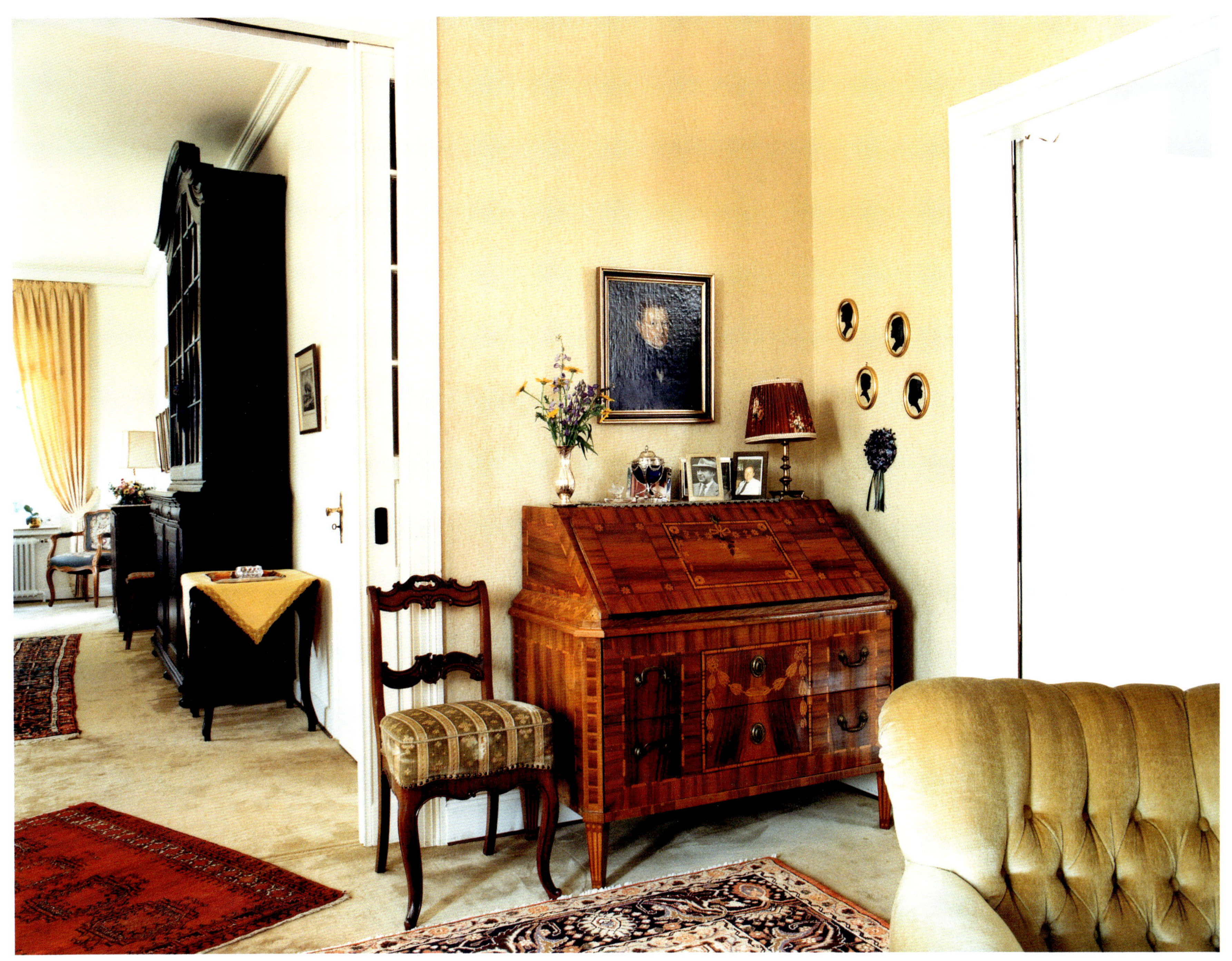

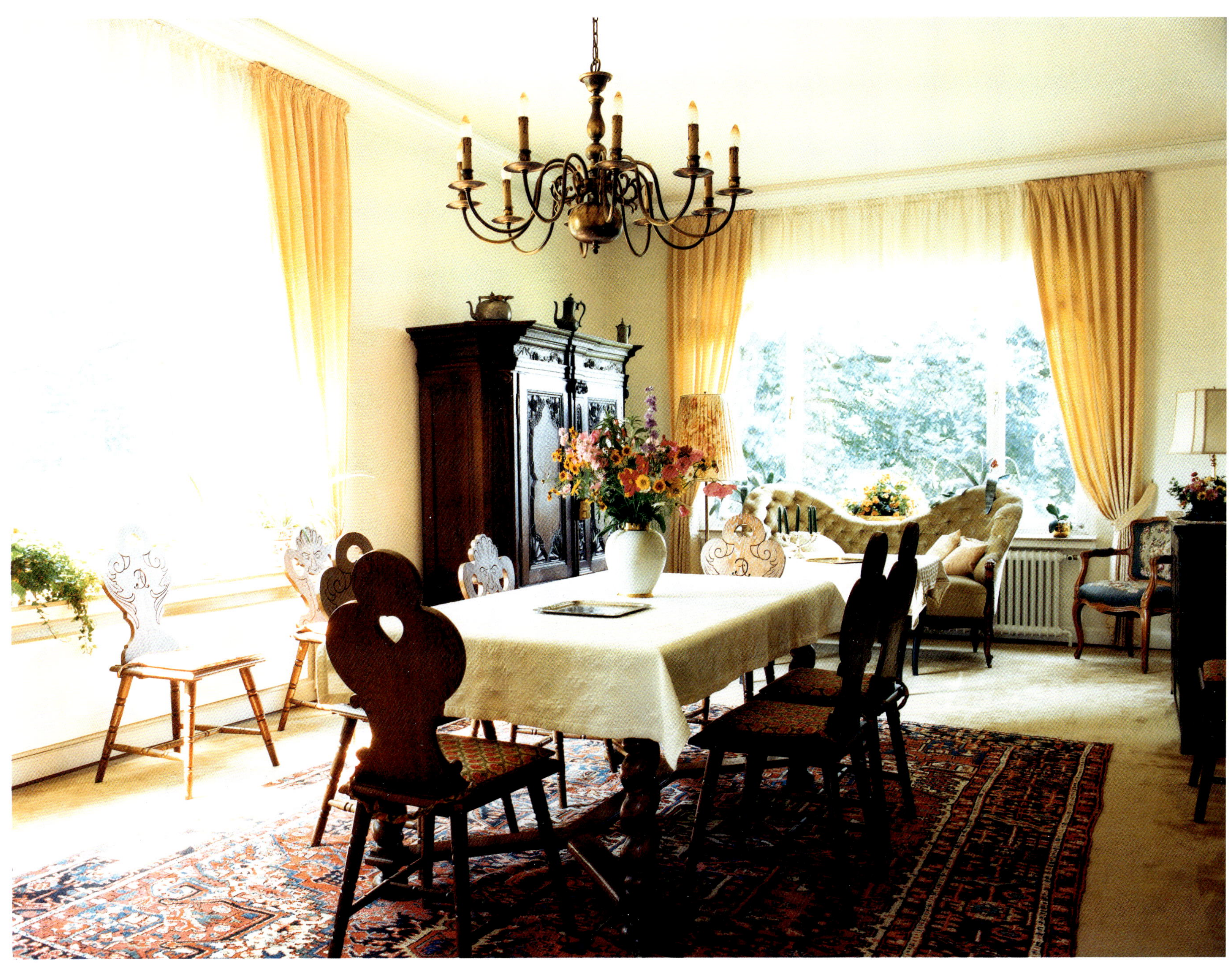

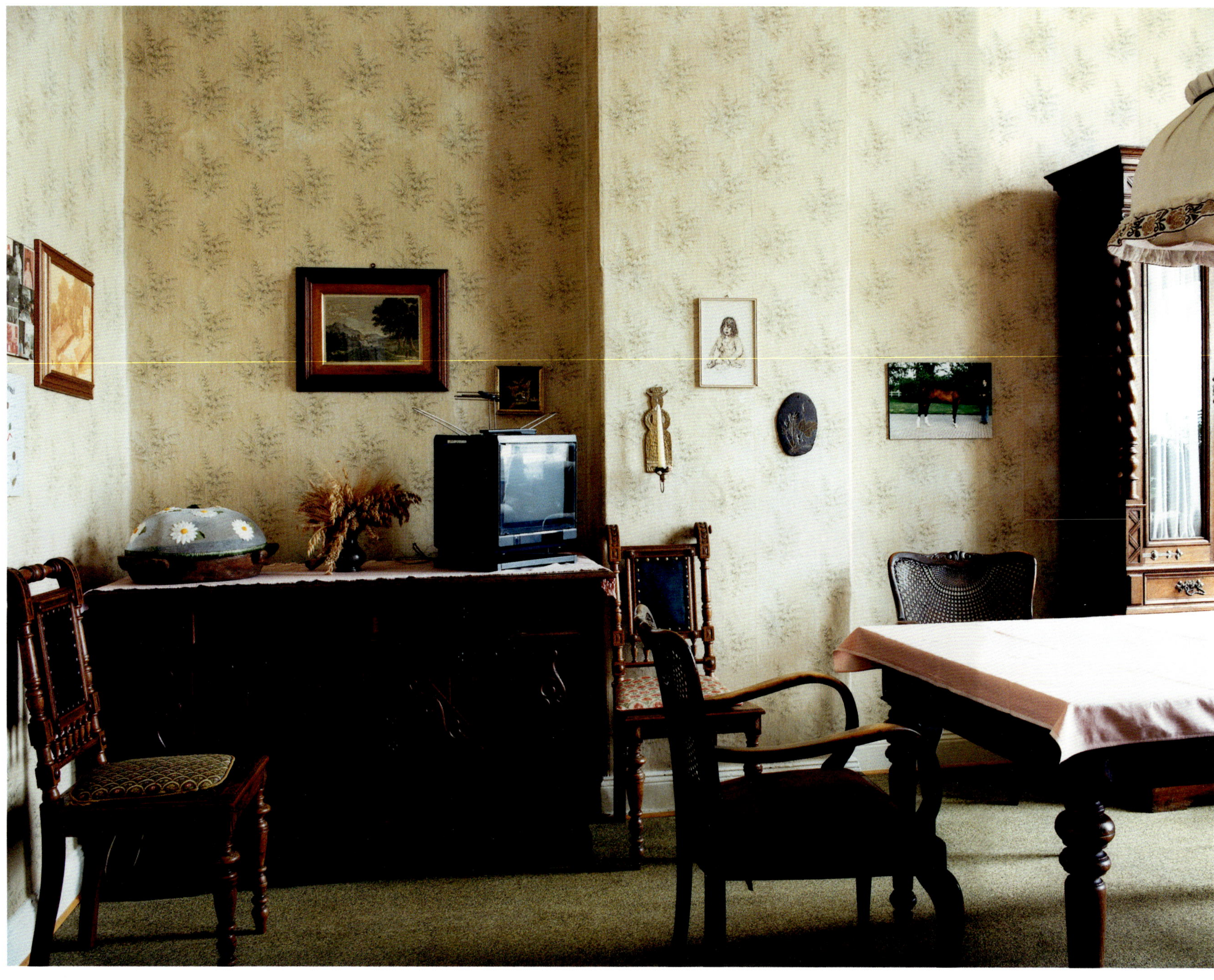

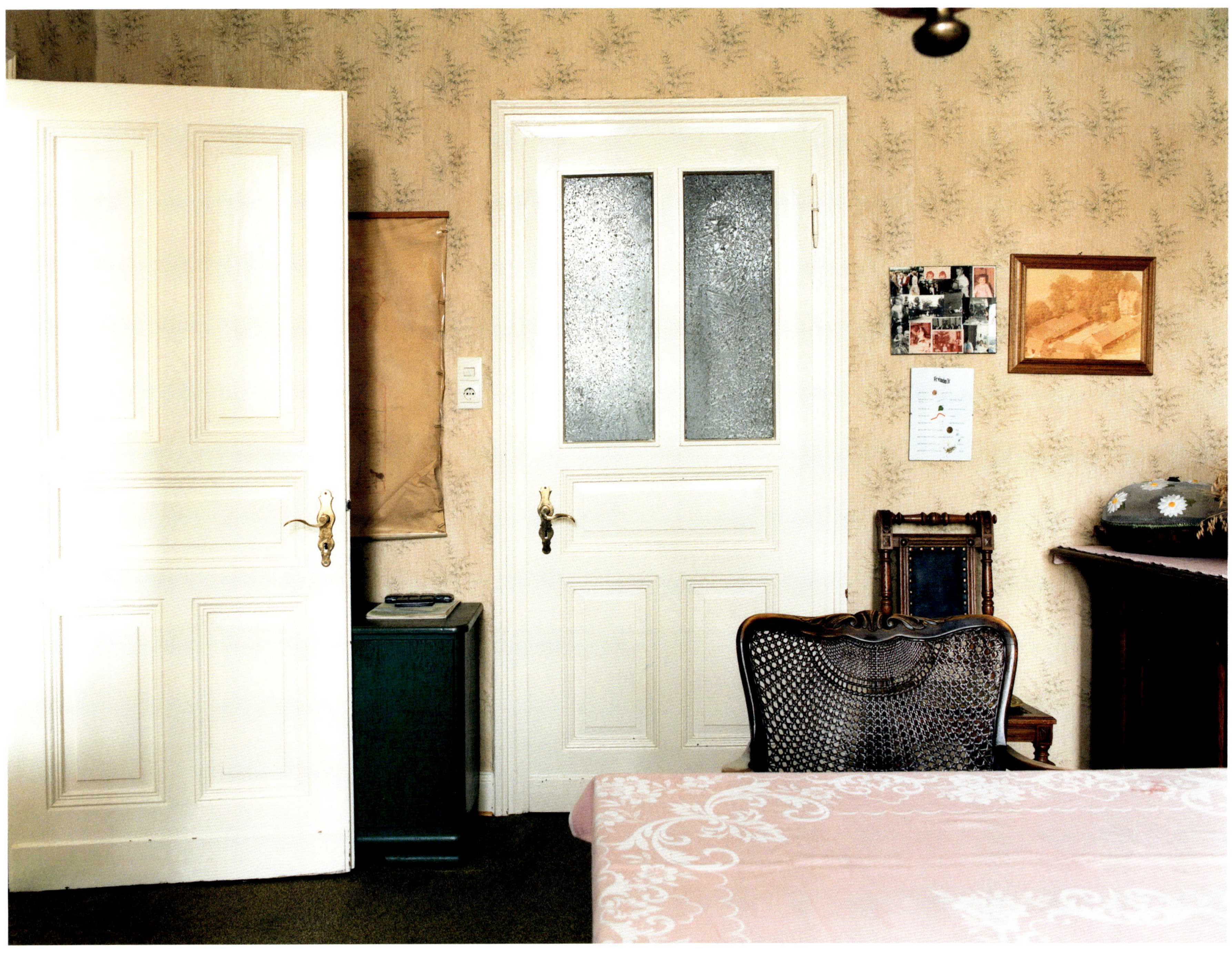

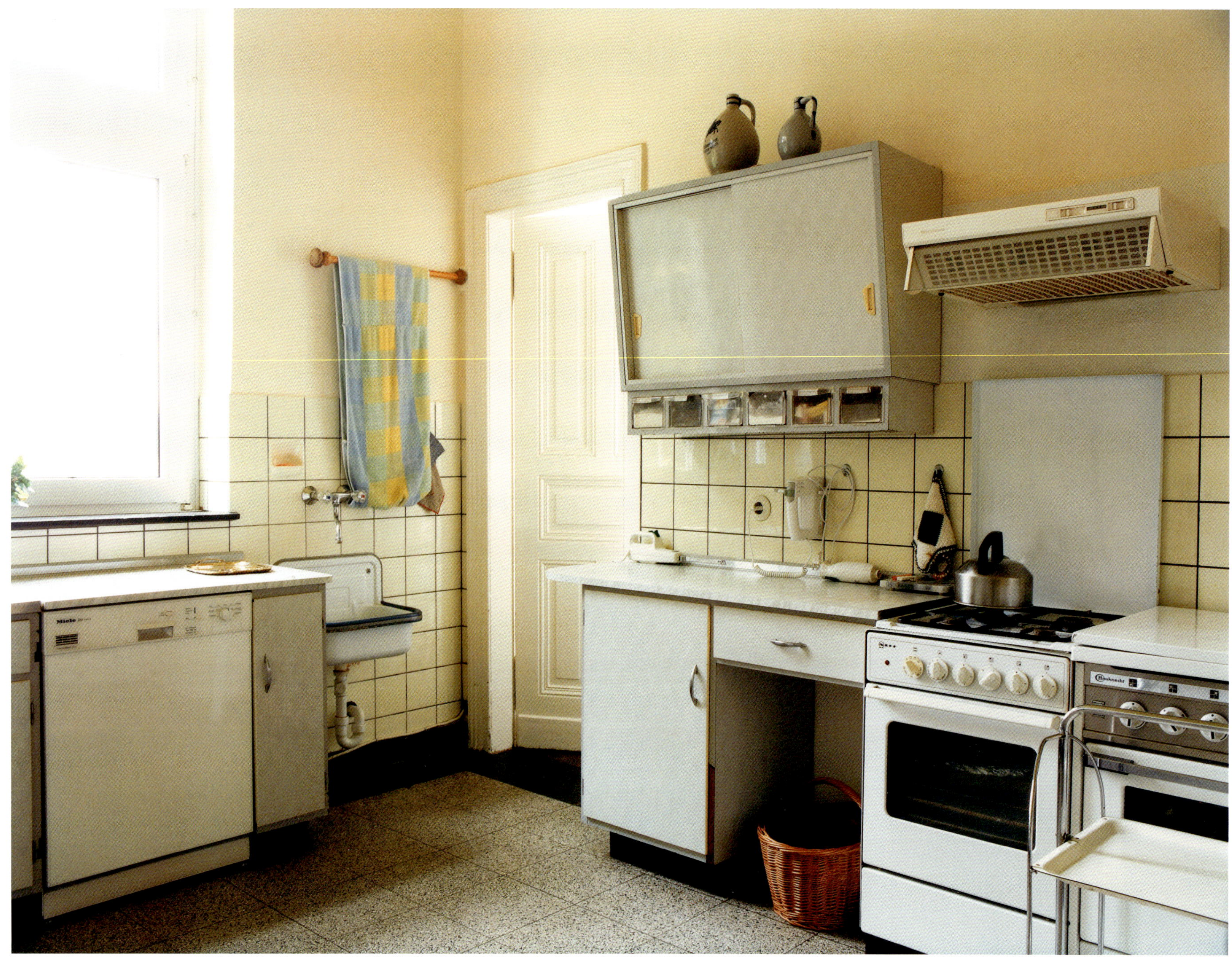

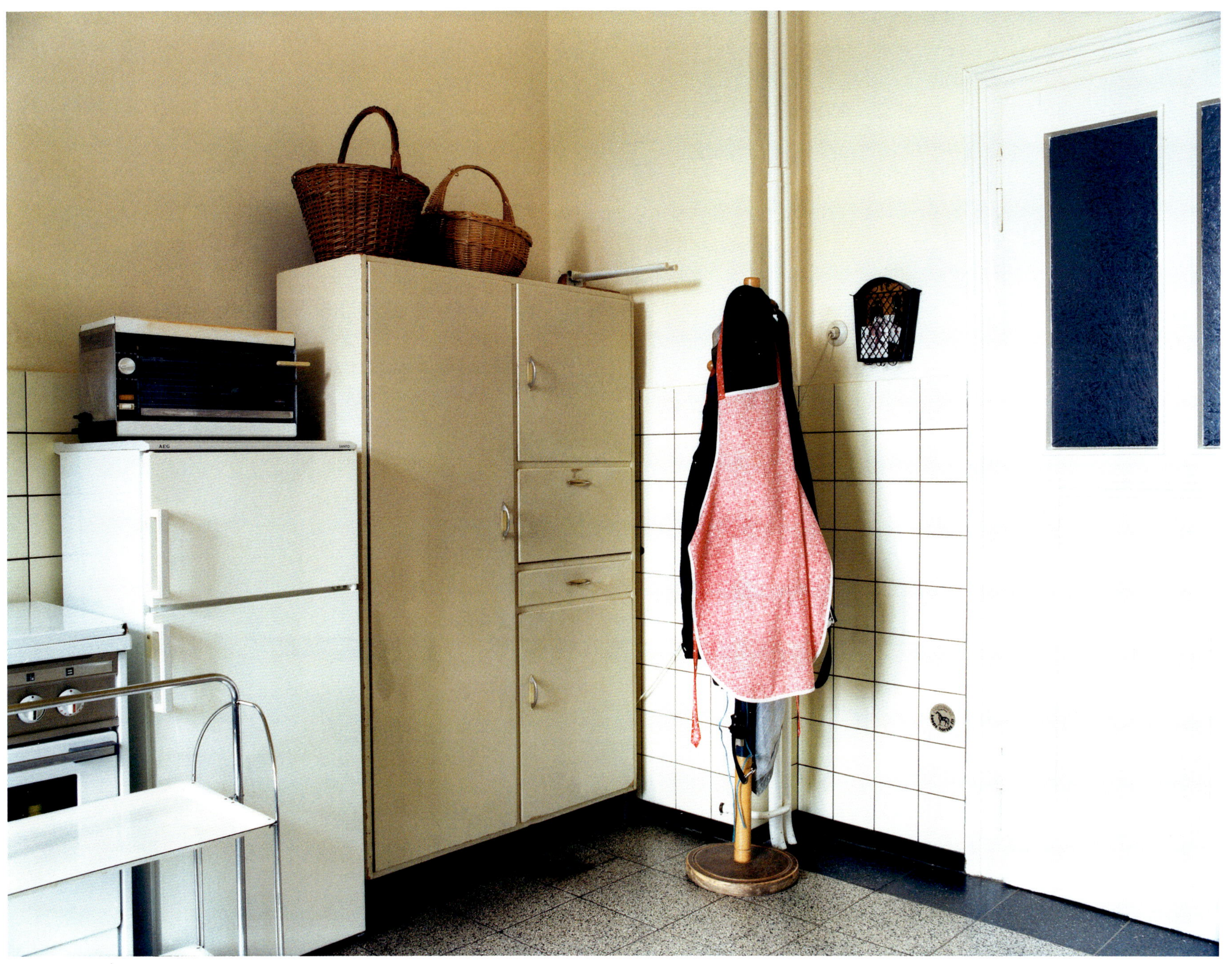
AEG

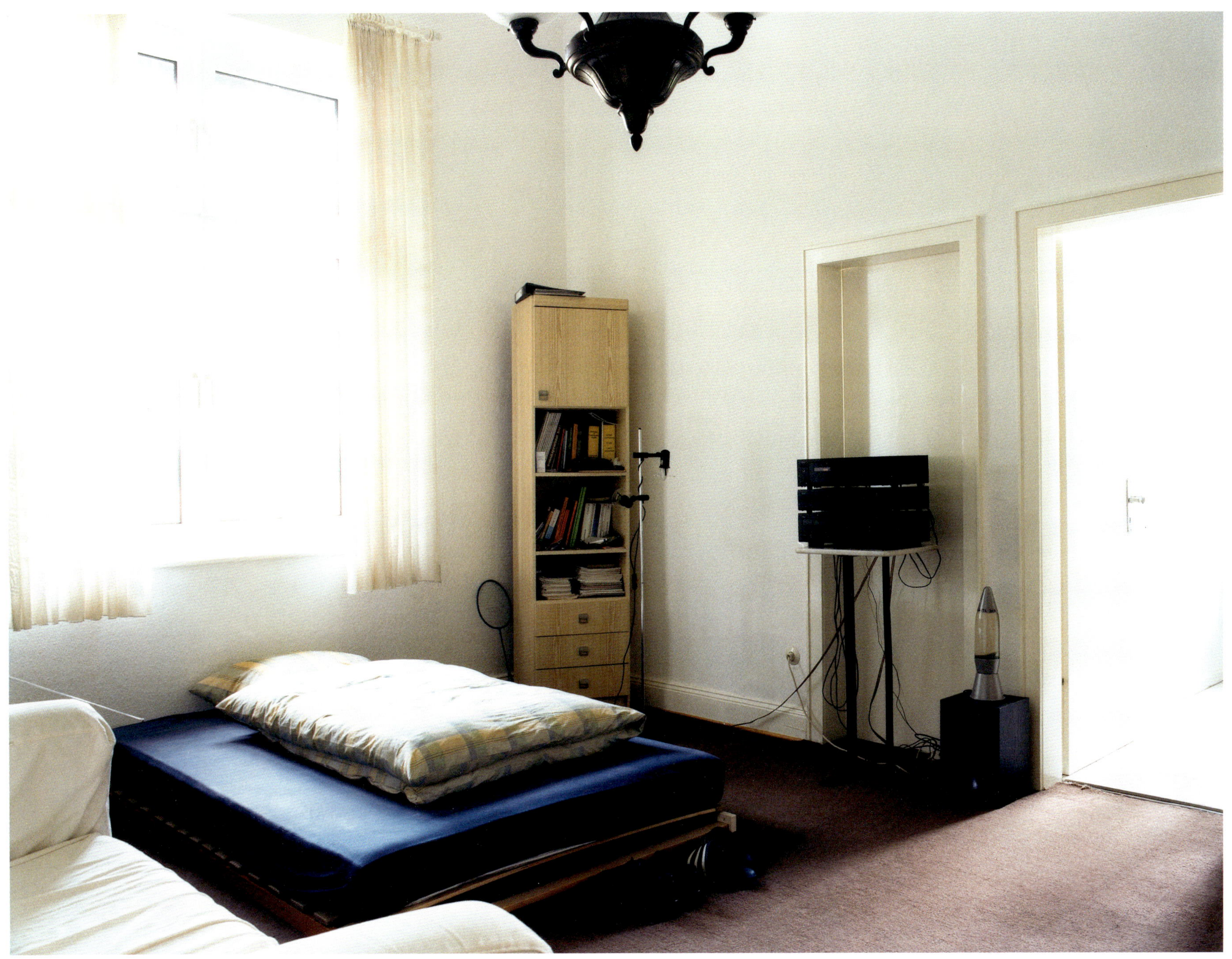

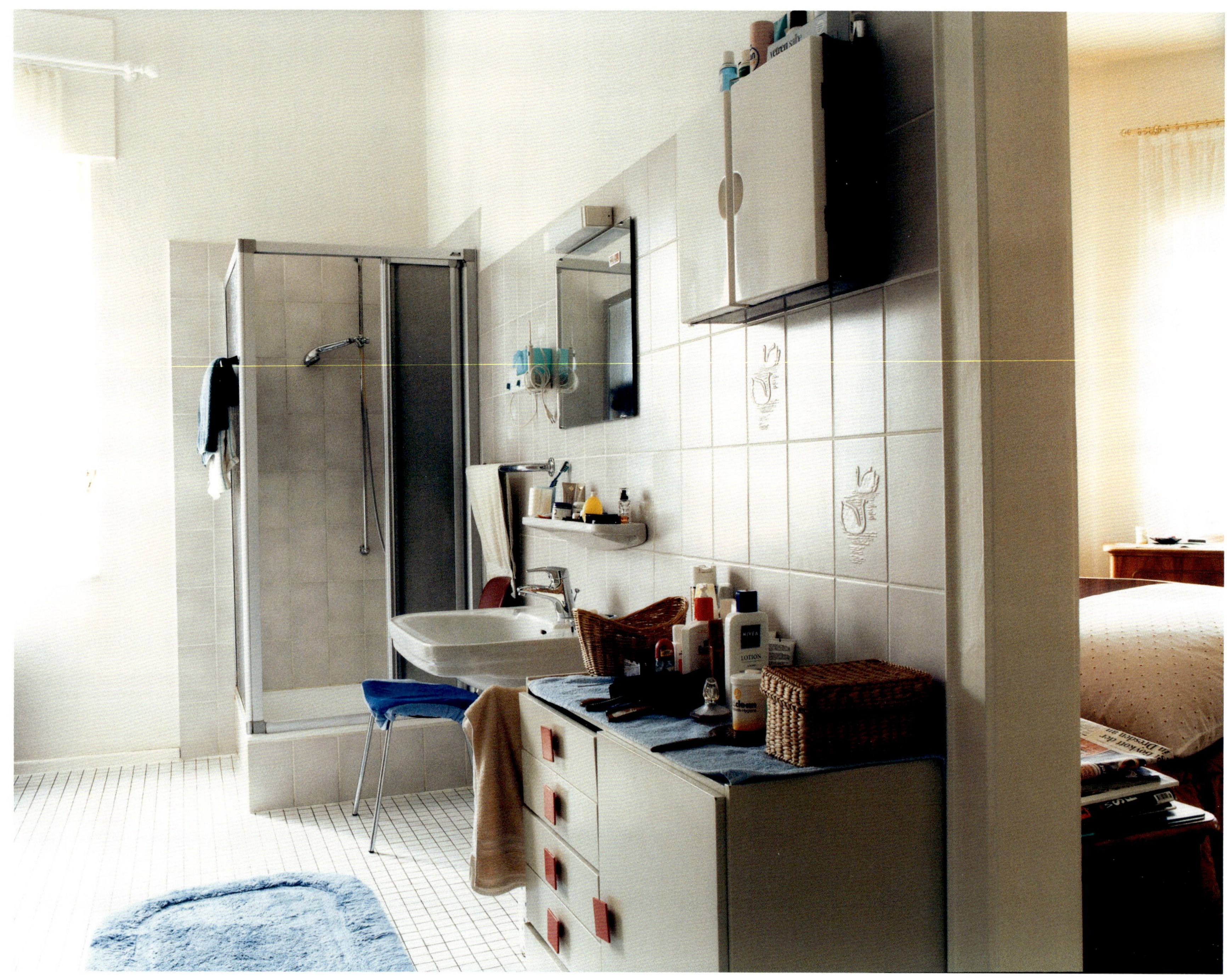

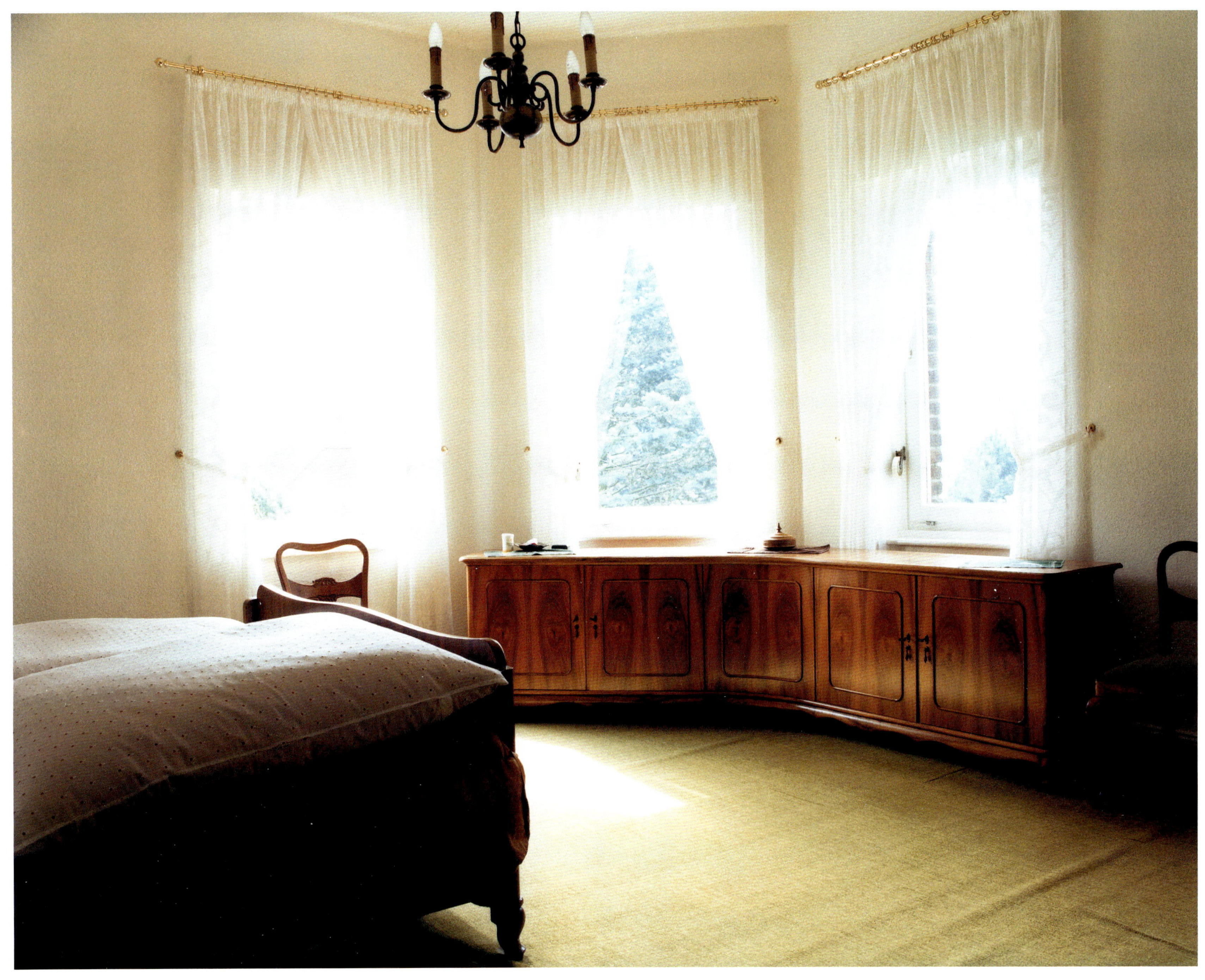

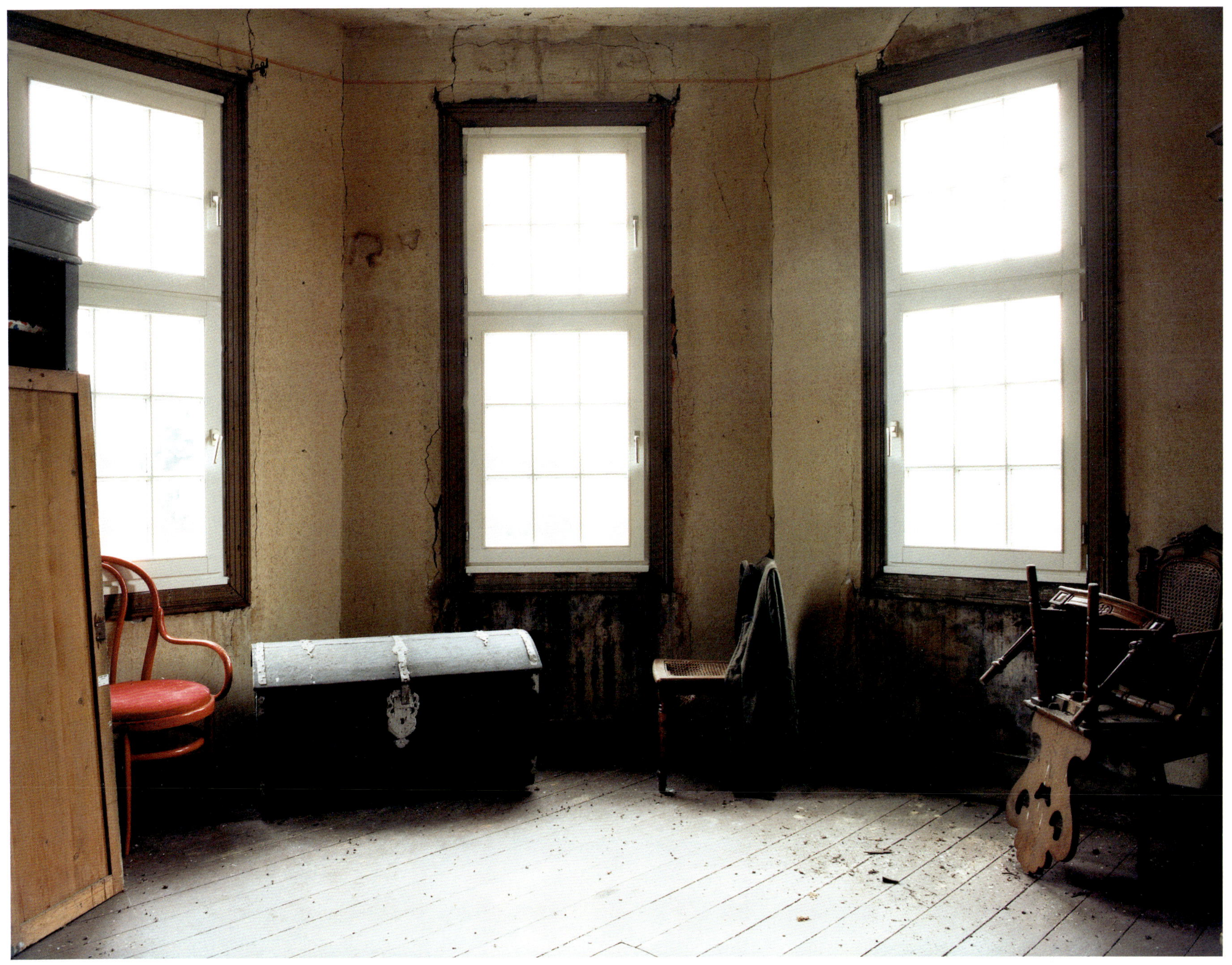

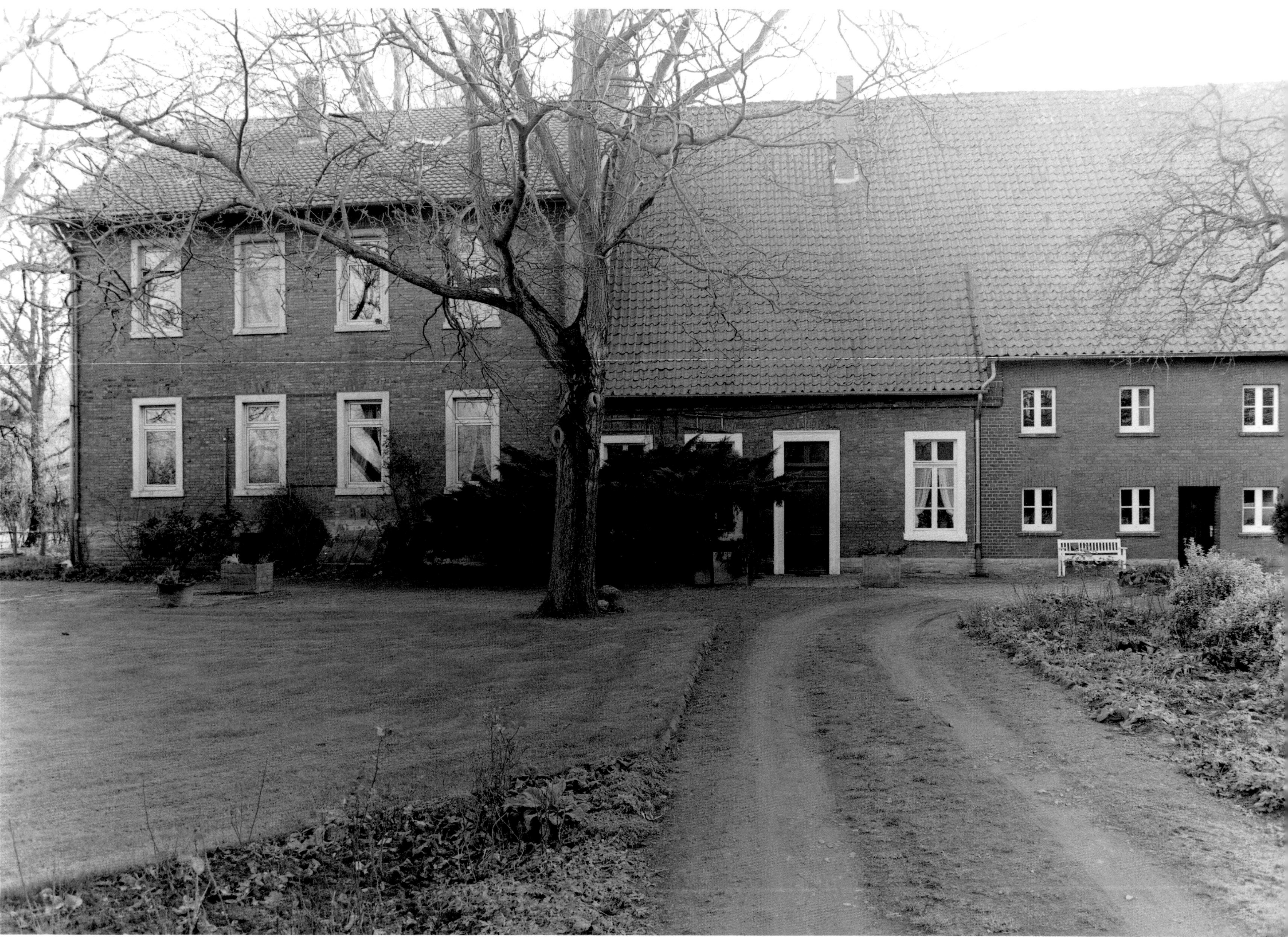

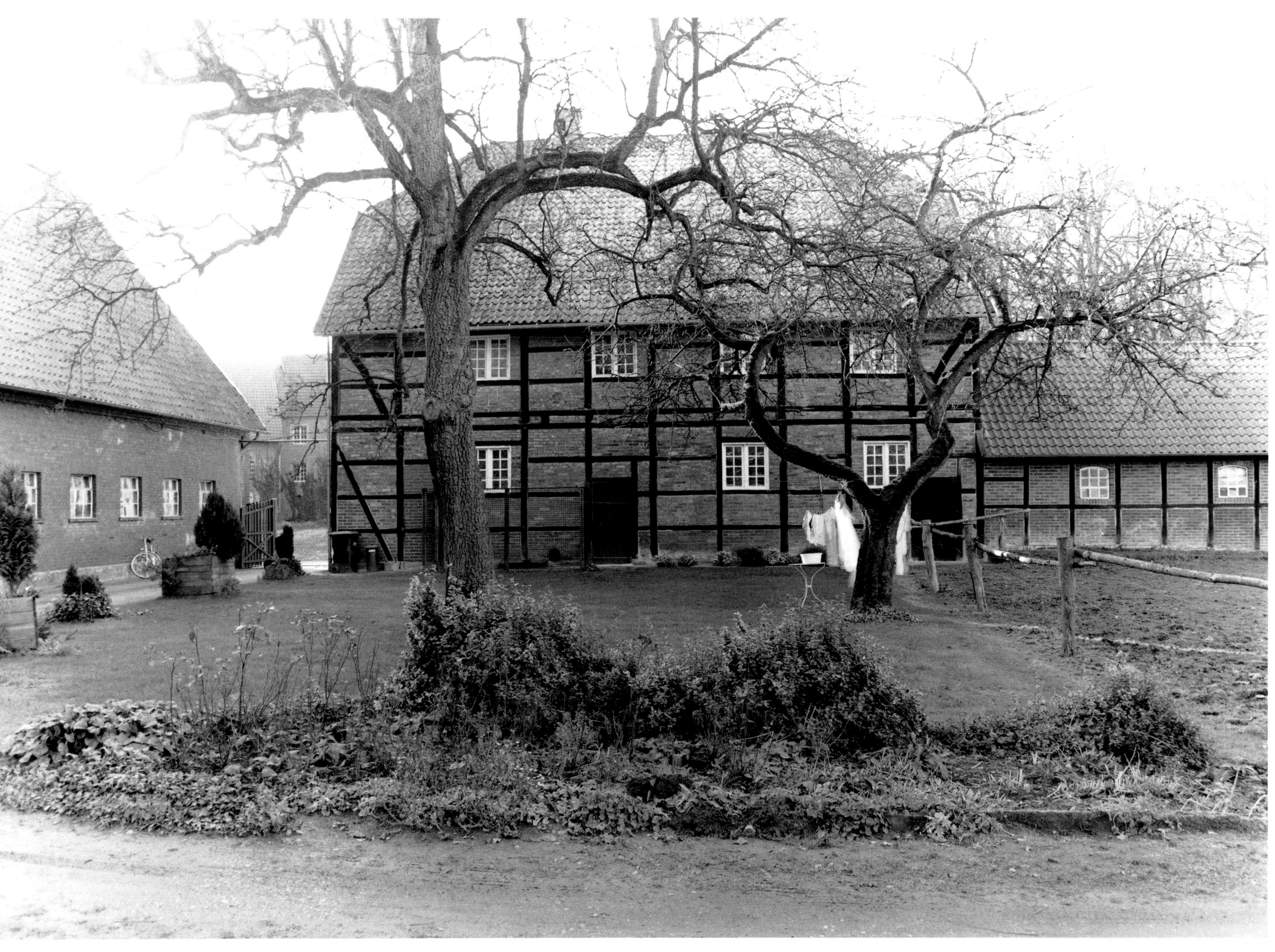

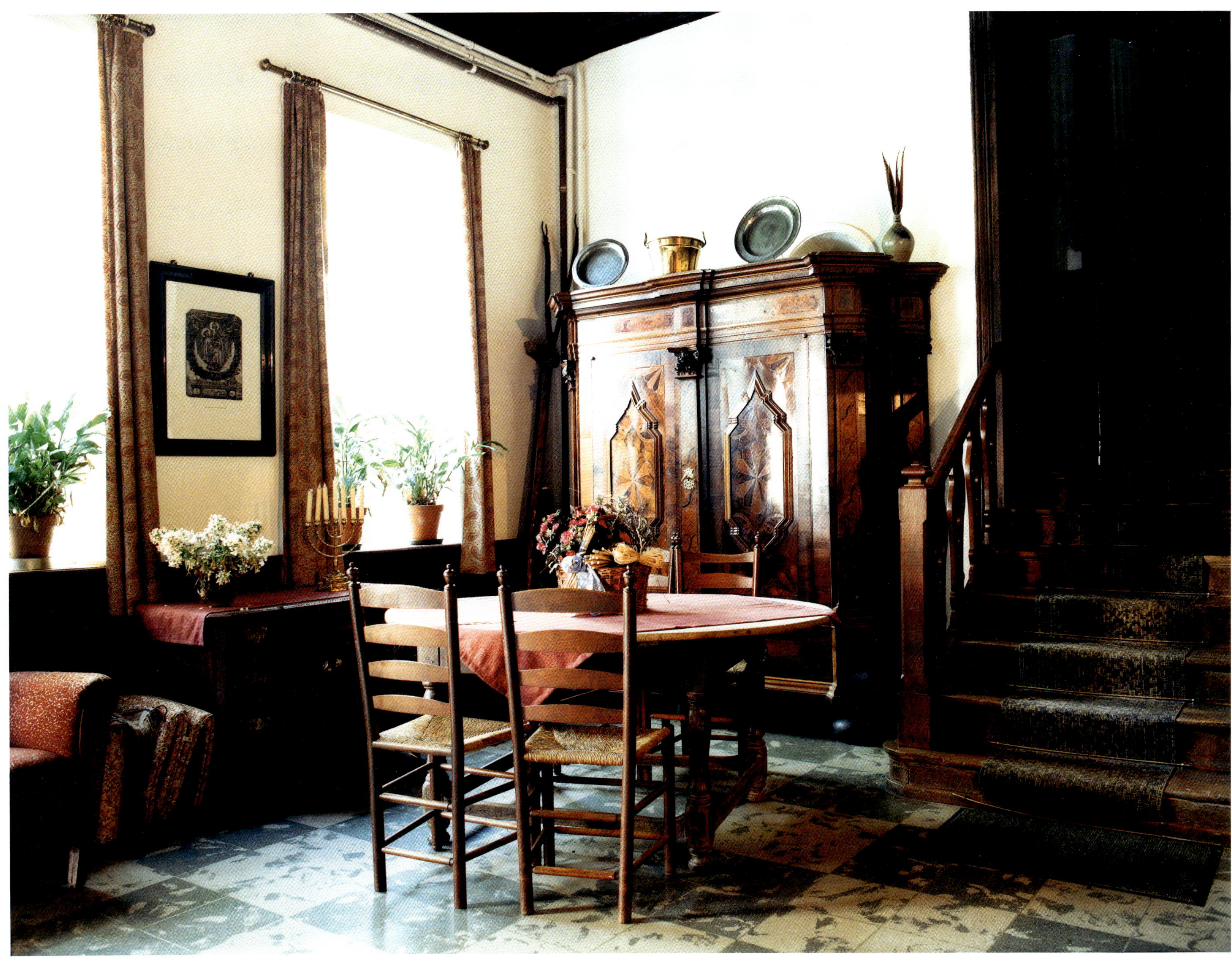

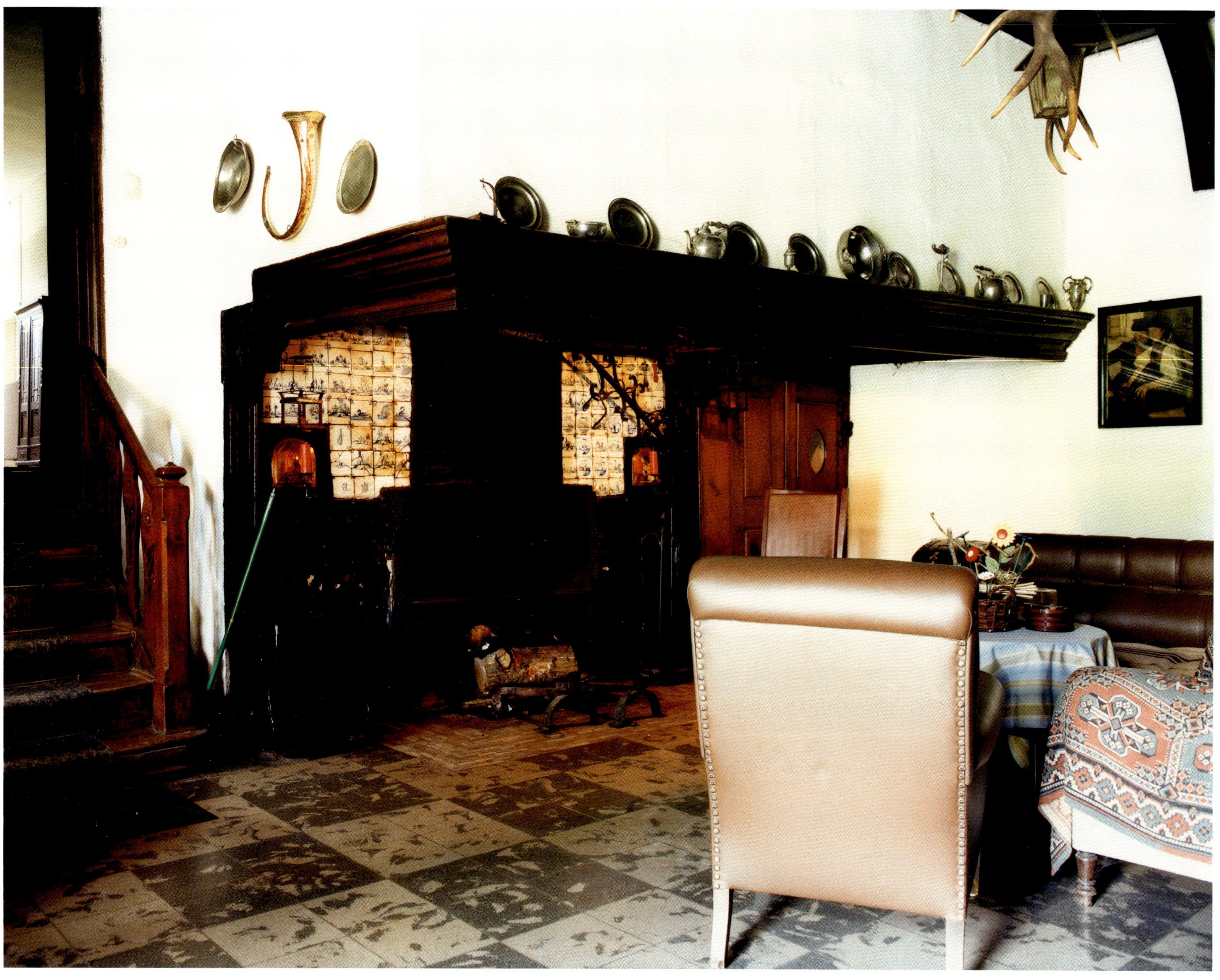

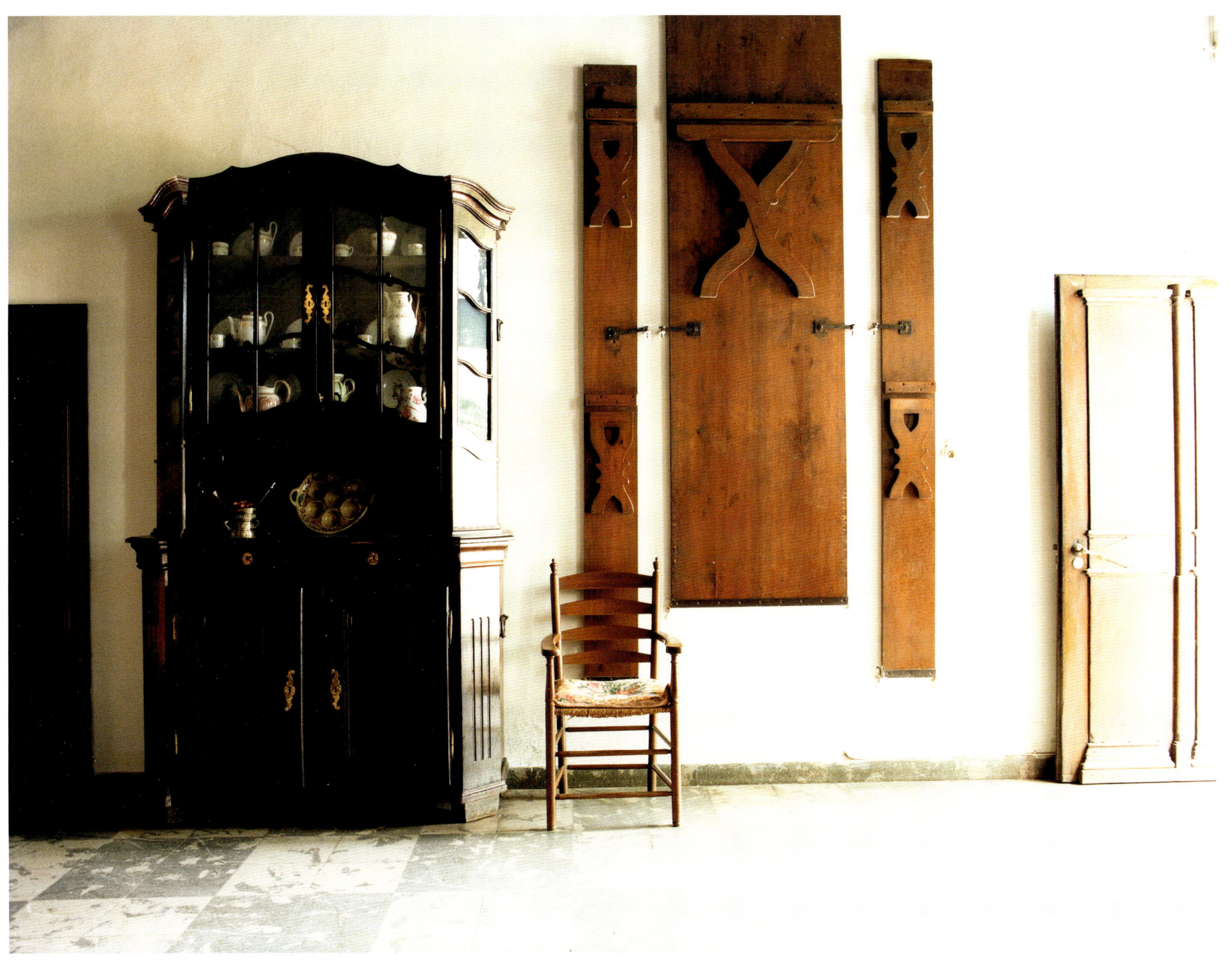

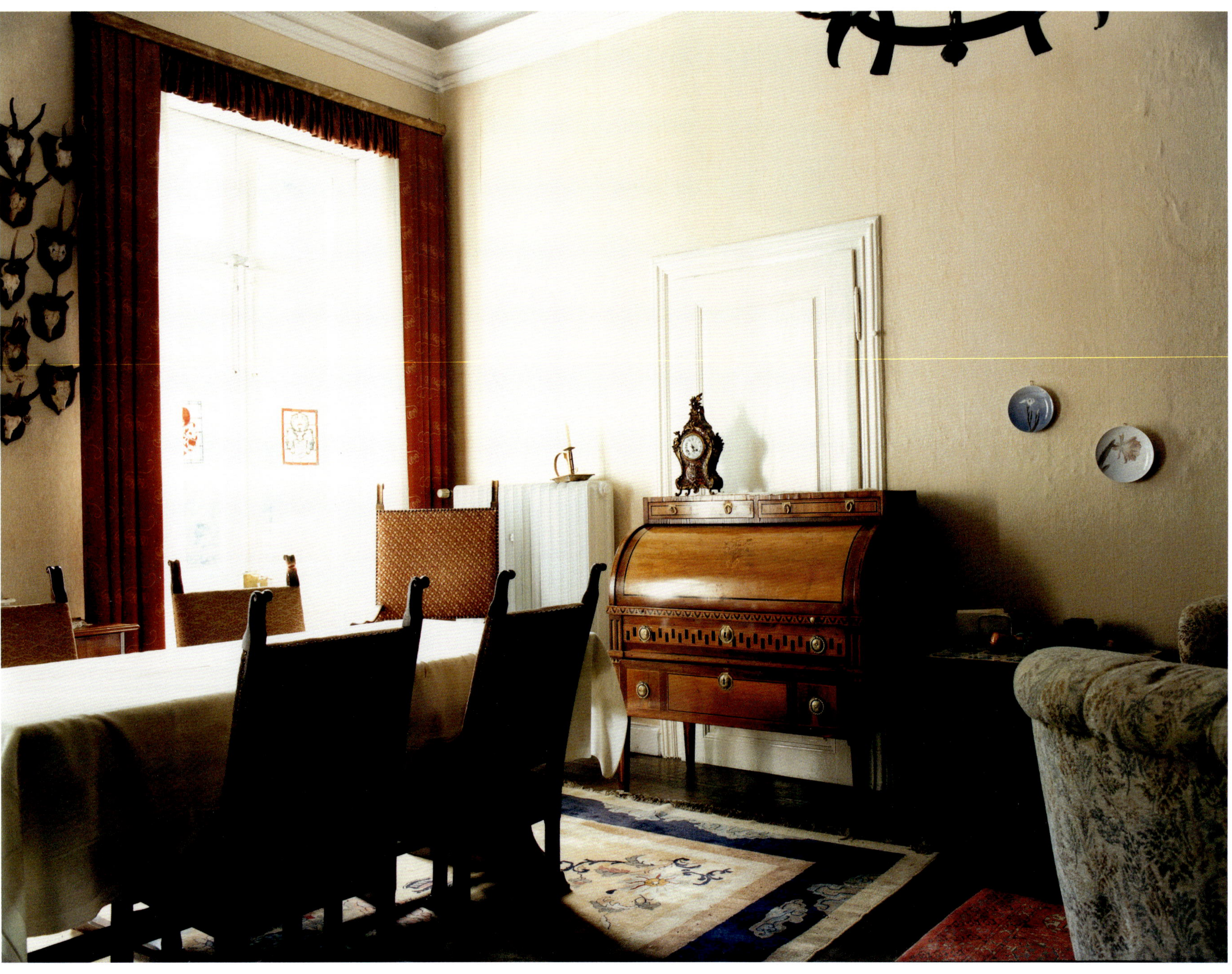

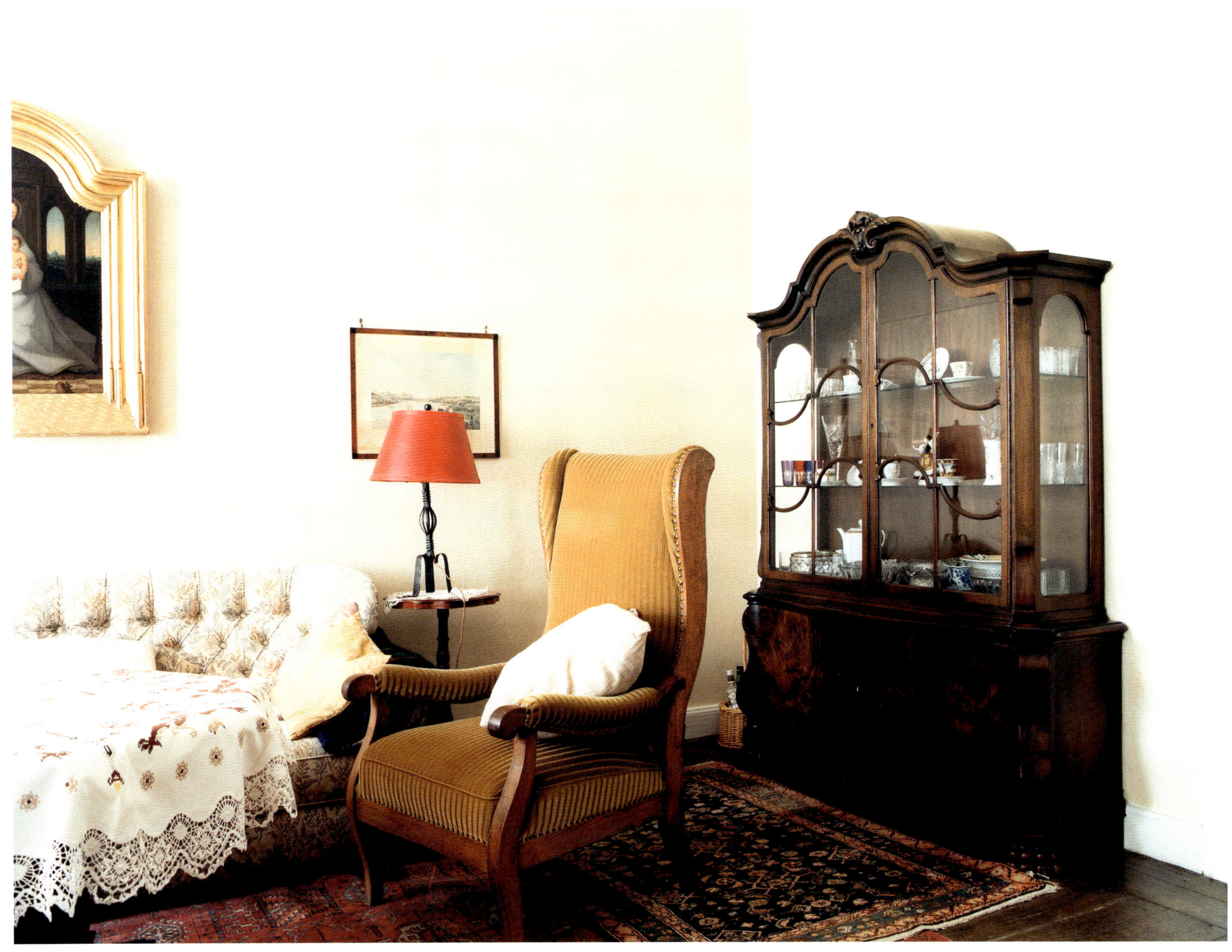

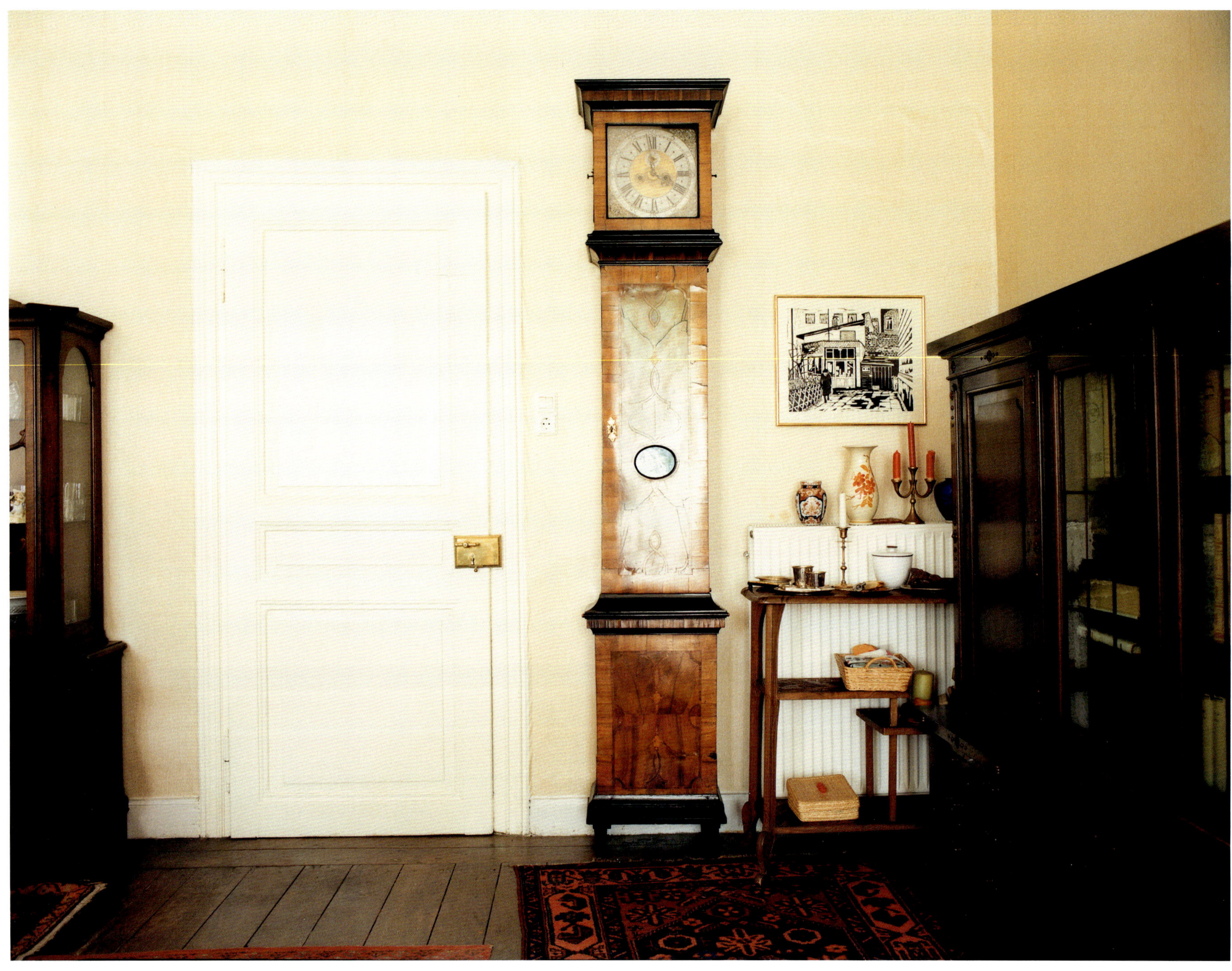

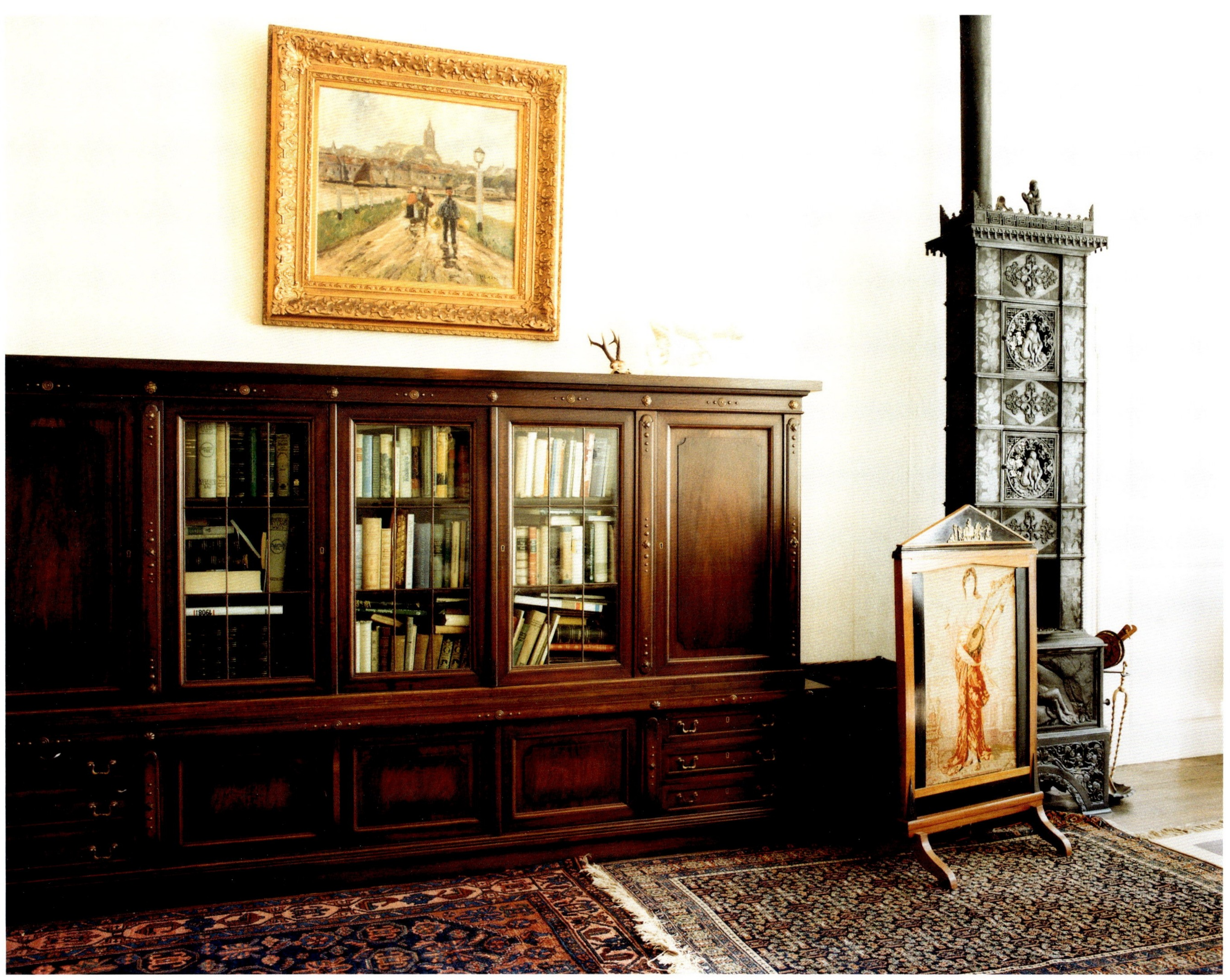

Jan Carstensen

inside – travelling with Martin Rosswog

It was a mildly cloudy day in May 1999, and the road from Münster stretched out lazily ahead of me. I was looking for one of the several large farms that populate this still quiet part of the country, with its expanses of fields and its marvellous, park-like cultural landscape. This area has lived from agriculture since the Middle Ages, practiced in the sparsely distributed farms. Behind a small oak forest, the road made a sharp bend to the left, and then suddenly, there I was, right in front of the gatehouse through which the inner courtyard could be seen, empty but for a dog that greeted me happily and a Citroën estate car with Rhineland number plates. Martin Rosswog was already there, true to plan, so I went in search of the doorbell, which I didn't find, but it didn't matter, because eventually somebody saw me and let me in. And so began my voyage of discovery through the large farms of the Münsterland, and of the people who live in them. Everything had been prepared as far as was practicably possible. We had arranged our spring day visit both by letter and by telephone. The hospitality displayed by our hosts was just right for beginning our photographic and documentary project on a happy note. But how did it all start?

First Meeting

I first encountered Martin Rosswog back in the 1980s. I met him in his home town of Lindlar in Oberberg. Right from the start, I was fascinated by his photographs, but I was no less impressed by Martin Rosswog the man. Around this time, I had just started working as an ethnologist at the local open-air museum, and it was clearly the ethnographic approach that he had to his work that inspired me. But it was more than that. I was also impressed by his single-mindedness in pursuing his goal, without paying a second thought to the art market. He had begun with portraits of subjects in his local region, which he extended continuously into thematically based series.[1] Later on, he travelled all over Europe, in search of traditional rural interiors, with the aim of documenting them in accordance with precisely laid down photographic principles and conditions. Only the German-speaking region is excluded from this approach. In the 1980s, the two of us searched for and found only a few examples of 'old-fashioned' living in the 'Bergisches Land' region.

More than ten years passed by, and I was now working in the Westphalian Open-Air Museum in Detmold; Martin Rosswog had been travelling through other countries on the edges of Europe, with the same constancy, when I re-established contact with him. I had been developing the field of photography into a major theme at the Detmold Museum, and strongly wished to initiate a joint project in the region of Westphalia. I succeeded in engaging Martin Rosswog's interest in the project. It became clear that the region of Westphalia as a whole was not sufficiently homogeneous for us to realistically pursue the project on such a scale, so we decided to concentrate on the typical 'Schultenhof' farms of the Münsterland.

Schulte Farms in Münsterland

In Münsterland, an owner of a large farm is known as a 'Schulte' or 'Schulze', but you won't find this word in the dictionary. However, if you look in the regional telephone directory, you will see that Schulte is a very common name, either alone or in composite forms. And this is not only the case here in the heart of Westphalia, but also across the northern Ruhr area and in the Sauerland.[2] The word 'Schulte' comes from the Old Saxon 'sculthetus', and is commonly encountered in the names of large, old farms, an example being Schulte-Bisping or 'the Schulte of the bishop'. The origin of its use in this way can be found in the medieval feudal system, which only came to a complete end here in the course of the nineteenth century. The farmers were not free to own their farms, since they were the property of the lords of the manor, who were members either of the nobility or the church. These farmers tended the land primarily as bonded labourers. In north-western Germany, this system of bonded labour was not quite as severe as in the areas east of the Elbe. A system of inheritance (whereby the farms were passed on in their entirety to the oldest, or, in some regions, the youngest son, and the remaining siblings received money) existed in Münsterland. In return, however, the farmers were required to supply hand and horse services to their lords. In the High Middle Ages, the farmer housed by the lord in a large, primary farm was known as a Schulte. The proprietor of the farm was required to collect the duties, in money and in kind, from the smaller farms in the region. Although this function was later performed by the lords' administrations themselves, the Schulte farms continued to occupy a higher position within the traditional structure of the agricultural society. As a result of the system of inheritance that was widespread in north-western Germany, the favourable agricultural economy, and the moderate tax burden on the farmers, a rich farming culture had begun developing in Westphalia by the beginning of the modern period.

The grand farmsteads and their often opulent interiors, with valuable furniture, pewter and textiles, represent a still visible expression of the former importance of the high rural class Schultes. This heritage is preserved and maintained today in many families.

Our small team[3] had declared its aim to find ten families from among this upper class of Westphalian farmers, who are still resident in a traditional Westphalian farmhouse, a Low German hall house similar to the Schultenhof farm that can be seen in the Westphalian open-air museum. But we soon realised that farming and family histories of the old farms in Westphalia were far more complex, and far more exciting, than we had expected. Only a few farming families still live in a traditional hall house.

From Farmhouse to Villa

The project began in 1999, focussing on the historical farmhouses of the open-air museum. Various approaches were taken – while Martin Rosswog was primarily interested in the apparently static conditions, which repeatedly placed him before new challenges, the ethnologist in the museum concerned himself with other questions: It is said that Westphalian farmers have considerable stamina and perseverance. Is it possible to find signs of earlier ways of life by examining the farms in existence today? What is it that is so special about the traditional dwelling culture of the Westphalian Schulte class? Is the way that the Schultenhof farm is presented in the museum completely accurate? The first stage of our research project into building and dwelling culture in the large farms of the Münsterland region was to create photographic documentation. The photographer declared a great interest in expanding his artistic creativity by dedicating himself to picturing these farms and the people that live in them.

A particularly good example is the so-called Schultenhof in the open-air museum:[4] The visitor enters the yard by passing through a gatehouse made of semi-timber. The yard is dominated by the large primary building of the Schulte-Bisping farm, from Alst near Albersloh, south of Münster, which was built in 1787. This grand, 42-metre-long building is a typical Low German hall house, as this form of farmhouse, that is common throughout the whole of north-western Germany, is known. It combines dwelling area, barns and crop storage facilities under a single roof. A gate at the gable end of the building leads to the large threshing floor, known in Westphalia as the 'Deele'. The stalls for the cows and the horses are positioned on either side of the *deele*. The harvested crops are stored in the huge loft above. The residential section of the house adjoins the end of the *deele* with a large kitchen, that was originally not walled off from the animal area. The open hearth lies in the middle of the room. In Münsterland, this takes the form of an open fire built into the wall with a large chimney hood, a design adopted from the nobility. In many cases, this hearth has remained a traditional central feature of the house until this day, even though it has long ceased being used for cooking purposes. Since the draughts coming in through the chimney made the fireplace uncomfortable to sit near at times, a swing-door partition began to be used in the eighteenth century, to separate the kitchen from the *deele*. This led to the typical, spacious kitchens of the Westphalian farmhouses, with their traditional dining area next to the fireplace. This area was always bright due to the large window nearby. Behind the hearth, at the other end of the house, there were other rooms and chambers. Side doors in the kitchen led to the garden and the well. Here were further outhouses, such as the bake-house, woodshed and granary.

Most Schulte farmers built themselves modern houses in the course of the nineteenth century. These were either extensions to the original farmhouse or, as in some cases, complete replacements. The basic reason for this development was the growing need for separate living from working areas. While a partition was deemed sufficient for this purpose at the end of the eighteenth century, the larger-scale farmer began building separate half-timber wings or two-storey brick houses as extensions to the old hall houses. By the turn of the twentieth century, spacious villas in historicism and art nouveau style started to become commonplace, in keeping with the growing need for prestige among the wealthy farming classes. Such grand houses continued to be built into the twentieth century, often resembling businessmen's city villa dwellings or rural manor houses.

By the time our project began drawing to a close, we had managed to peg out the central stages in the development of rural dwellings in Münsterland from the hall house to the countryside villa. We decided that our tenth and final example should be a building from the present, to ensure that our presentation did not end at a some point in the middle of the historical developments. We therefore selected a house for documentation from the year 1995. This brought our study up-to-date by pursuing building developments right up until the present day. However, it was still possible to see clear signs of the former dwelling styles in the modern buildings through the inherited furnishings that were clearly still in use.

The Present in the Museum

In parallel to the Schultenhof project, the open-air museum began conducting research into the dwelling culture of the present day. In a project entitled 'RoomWorlds, how young people live today', we documented the current dwellings of the young generation, focussing on their immediate environment and the objects that surround them at the turn of the 21st century. The result of this project was an exhibition in the year 2000, that garnered praise nationally.[v] Interestingly, comparisons of these and the children's rooms in both projects revealed numerous similarities.

In contrast to the RoomWorlds project, in which many young people were involved, no systematic interviews have as yet been carried out in the Schulte families. Yet both projects have something in common: they are both concerned with present living situations, and how to document these tellingly for generations to come. The main aspect is not so much the static material but more the effort required in making choices from the wide range of possibilities, in such a way as to give as broad a representation as possible. It is clear, and it will not be denied here, that a certain degree of randomness is required to do this. The selection was performed in conversation between the artist and the academic. The criteria were the house forms in which the Schulte families live, and not least the wish expressed by the museum to gain as deep an insight as possible into the traditional, rural social stratum.

Thanks to his artistic meticulousness and perseverance, Rosswog succeeded in creating a visual reminder of European dwelling culture that stands out in its uniqueness. His series show an exemplary repertoire of both new furnishings and items from between the 1930s and the present, in which old, inherited pieces of furniture have been integrated. Such milieus of the second half of the twentieth century have so far hardly ever been documented in such a context, or systematically gathered in the form of original items for the benefit of future generations – an important job for culture-historical museums. But it is not only the fact that Martin Rosswog's work is interesting from an ethnographic and museum-based point of view, but his working procedures and methods are also worthy of further examination.

The Photographic Series

'The photographer Martin Rosswog is an artistic documentary maker'. This is how Andreas Graf chooses to begin his introduction to the most comprehensive book so far written about Rosswog's photographs of rural interiors in Europe.[6] Graf then goes on to describe the working methods and procedures of the photographer in great detail: Rosswog's first trip took him to Ireland in 1989, where he would return several times in the following years. Ireland was followed by Spain in 1992 and Finland in 1995; again he also undertook subsequent visits in order to complete his series. Fittingly, the book describes Rosswog's interest in 'cultural islands'.[7] The large farms can also be regarded as constituting a cultural island by way of their uniqueness within their surrounding environment as well as their social standing.

Cultural islands such as these have always been a source of interest for Bernd and Hilla Becher, and Rosswog was a master pupil of theirs. Comparisons with their work illustrate clearly what the two approaches have in common, and also the areas in which Rosswog is going his own way. The well-known Becher tableaux, containing photographs of semi-timber buildings, have been looked into in great detail.[8] An essential factor of creative activity is the arrangement of photographs in such a way that the meaning of each individual picture recedes into the background.[9] A similar phenomenon can also be observed in Rosswog's photographs in the Schulte project. While each interior photograph, from a folkloristic point-of-view, can first of all be viewed as an enrichment of the research material, this is not enough for him. He adjoins one image to another, determining precisely which two, three, four or five images belong together, which should be hung up at a fitting distance to each other, while still maintaining their association. While the Bechers' tableaux can comprise nine pictures, in a three by three formation, a Rosswog series can easily comprise between two and six pictures, while he has also composed series of 2 + 3 and 5 + 1 photographs. Single images are often strongly centred images or details taken from a larger series. These series are not random, but they contain optical 'joins', to allow the observer, if he is prepared to look closer, to work out where they fit together. These interassociations are created by way of furniture or doors and windows; these are viewed from different perspectives and in different positions within the photographs. Nevertheless, it is possible, indeed it is Rosswog's intention, that a series of five, for instance, can also be reduced to a smaller series of two, while retaining its validity. Many pictures are powerful as individual images, but they take on an extra dimension in the context of the other pictures in the series. Some require solitude to take on their full effect between two series. This power that the images emit has been taken into consideration while planning the book. In particular when photographing small rooms, Rosswog positions himself very close to the wall, in his endeavour to capture as much of the interior as possible. The light wide-angle lens he uses is particularly effective in achieving this. In contrast, his exterior images can be in the form of panoramas, an effect which corresponds with his recording of the embedded nature of the farms in their rural environment. Only in these outside photographs does he make use of both black-and-white and colour film material. The interiors are always in colour and the portraits all in black-and-white. Like the Bechers, Rosswog attempts to remove as many shadows as possible from the image by choosing long exposures combined with diffuse illumination.[10] A vivid cloudscape would be out of place in a Rosswog image. Inasmuch as it is possible to categorise Rosswog's images, they are, if anything, defined by their various room functions: dwelling, cooking, ironing, writing, sleeping, bathing, storing, and placing.

A continuous feature of our project is the region of Münsterland. From the various ages of the residents and the changing family constellations, the occasions and time points could be seen at which changes had been made in the past to the fittings in the room. A common cause of change to the interior design were weddings and the generation change that these bring about – just as can be observed in other places too. Unlike his trips to the outer regions of Europe, in which Rosswog sought out and found only older people, living alone, in Münsterland, we mostly encountered families of varying sizes: mothers and grown-up sons, parents with young or older children, or even three generations under the same roof. These families resemble our more common social conditions more closely than do the people that form the subjects of Rosswog's work in other countries. It is perhaps so that it is easier for us to recognise things from our own lives in these pictures. The observer may be quite surprised to see how the residents here attempt to expose their personal aesthetic. Clearly, the need for symmetry plays an important role here. But it is in particular these combinations of old and new, of valuable antiques and modern furnishings from the discount store, of tidiness and messiness, in close proximity to one another, that renders the everyday life pictured here all the more visible.

This intimate insight into the people's current lives is not only of interest to cultural scientists, but parallels can already be seen in the current photography scene, and even a number of successors. For example, there is now a 'Helsinki School' comprising a young generation of photographers who have succeeded in gaining considerable recognition in Finland, as well as in other countries.[11] They orient themselves, as they themselves admit, towards the Becher school. Do they also have Rosswog's work in their sights, and will they go on to focus more on series? Certainly, Rosswog's photographs were exhibited in Helsinki and Tampere in 1997. It remains to be seen where these exciting developments will lead.

'inside houses'

Both for this book and for the Detmold exhibition entitled: *inside* – Schultenhöfe des Münsterlandes' the artist has selected and arranged a number of important images from the project as a whole.[12] Allow these pictures to speak to you directly, and you will see that they are addictive. It is a visual addiction that arises if you are prepared to take part in the experiment, which requires you to adopt the sight and the vision of the photographer for a short while. If you look closely at the photographs, you will see the objects of everyday life with other eyes. In his photographs, Martin Rosswog documents the traditional dwelling culture of Europe with a density of form and content whose value only becomes apparent when compared with the images presented today by the media. This may be due to the fact that these photographs represent an ideal combination of art and documentation. Once you are captivated by these places and rooms, you feel you want to take others with you on this journey – and that is the purpose of both the book and the exhibition. So adopt the *'inside'* perspective – just as promised in the title of the exhibition – and take part in a research project that turns privacy into the point of departure for a creative, artistic process.

1 *Menschenbilder: Porträtfotografien von Martin Rosswog.* (Dumont Verlag) Cologne 1989. And very recent 'Heritage – Fotografien von Martin Rosswog' in the Rheinische Landesmuseum Bonn, (Schirmer/Mosel) Munich 2005.

2 Leopold Schütte: 'Schulte und Meier in (Nordost-)Westfalen', in: *Spieker – Landeskundliche Beiträge und Berichte* 37, Münster 1995, pp. 211-225.

3 The team also includes the genealogist Jörg Wunschhofer (from Beckum), to whom I would like to express my sincere thanks.

4 See museum guide: *Westfälisches Freilichtmuseum Detmold – Landesmuseum für Volkskunde.* Detmold 2001, pp. 104-110 and also Heinrich Stiewe: 'Vom Umgang mit Häusern im Museum', in: Stefan Baumeier and Jan Carstensen (eds.): *Westfälisches Freilichtmuseum Detmold. Geschichte – Konzepte – Entwicklungen.* Detmold 1996, pp. 69-108; here p. 75ff.

5 Jan Carstensen, Thomas Düllo, Claudia Richartz-Sasse (eds.): *ZimmerWelten – Wie junge Menschen heute wohnen. Schriften des Westfälischen Freilichtmuseums Detmold 23.* Essen 2000.

6 Andreas Graf: 'Die Kunst erfinden und verbergen', in: Martin Rosswog: *Inside Houses. Rural Homes in Europe/ Ländliches Wohnen in Europa/ Maisons rustique en Europe.* Cologne 2001, pp. XI-XVIII, here p. XI.

7 Graf 2001 (see 6 above), p. XVII.

8 Martina Dobbe: *Bernd und Hilla Becher, Fachwerkhäuser.* Museum der Gegenwartskunst Siegen, series of papers, vol. 1, Siegen 2001.

9 Dobbe 2001 (see 8 above), p. 29.

10 Dobbe 2001 (see 8 above), p. 42.

11 *The Helsinki School. Photography by TaiK, issued by the University of Art and Design Helsinki.* Ostfildern 2005.

12 A catalogue containing approximately 500 black-and-white and colour images has been published to coincide with the 'Schultenhöfe' project. Of these, 150 photographs were purchased from the Westfälisches Freilichtmuseum Detmold. The dimensions of the black and white images are approximately 27 x 38 cm, those of the colour images approximately 22 x 30 cm.

Dieses Buch erscheint anlässlich der Ausstellung

[inside] – Schultenhöfe des Münsterlandes
Fotografien von Martin Rosswog

Westfälisches Freilichtmuseum Detmold
– Landesmuseum für Volkskunde –
(Landschaftsverband Westfalen-Lippe)
14. Juni – 30. Oktober 2005

Konzeption des Bildteils: Martin Rosswog
Übersetzung ins Englische: Atlas Übersetzungsbüro, Bochum

Herstellung der Farbfotografien: Fachlabor Wagner, Bergisch Gladbach
Lithografie: NovaConcept, Berlin
Druck und Bindung: Passavia Druckservice, Passau

ISBN 3-8296-0206-5 (Buchhandelsausgabe)
Eine Schirmer/Mosel-Produktion
www.schirmer-mosel.com